For God's Sake, **Think Social Engagement...**

not just 'likes' and 'shares'!

Ashwin Razdan

Vitasta

Let Knowledge Spread

Published by
Vitasta Publishing Pvt. Ltd.
2/15, Ansari Road, Daryaganj,
New Delhi - 110 002
info@vitastapublishing.com

ISBN 978-93-80828-87-9

Cover Design by Aarti Vasudevan
Layout Design by Vitasta Publishing Pvt. Ltd.
Printed by Vits Press, New Delhi

Dedicated with much love and
affection to my beloved grandfather
Shri M L Razdan

APPRECIATION QUOTES

"A completely new and refreshing perspective on combining marketing with social media to get the best for both. This is truly a modern approach."

— **Dr Sunil Ashra**
Chairperson, School of Energy Management
Associate Professor (Economics)
Management Development Institute

☙❧

"In the era of Social media and two way communication, conventional marketers are going back to black boards to learn and redefine the approach. Market leaders become obsolete and new comer can potentially become role model. The days of progressive evolution of knowledge are gone. The disruption requires fast learning and adoption, innovation and experimentation to harness the benefit of the new rapidly expanding, 100% connected social channel.

Brand going viral (of course for good reason) is the dream of marketers today! Millions are spend on TV ads, in free give always to get sizable mass connected to the social handles. Some of these will write history and some of them will become history!"

— **Rohan Sinha**
Vice President–Transitions
Aegis Limited

ℭℬℭ

"Increasingly Social Media is becoming an important part of many integrated campaigns. The need to leverage it to the fullest has never been greater. This book gives an excellent insight into how brands should start thinking about it, and work towards building a formula for success. Overall, a good read."

— **Alok Agrawal**
COO
Cheil India/SW Asia Regional HQ

CONTENTS

FOREWORD

It seems like just a few days ago that content and communication was a one way street. Content that the information consumer received was what the editorial high priests felt was good for them. In most cases it was opinionated and it seemed like the intent was more to influence than inform. Those were the *not so long ago* days when print media reigned supreme. Consumers/readers who had an opinion or a grouse or a suggestion would write in to high priests who in turn would decide what was and wasn't good to carry. It seems like a few hours ago the internet came in to our lives and that changed the way we consumed content but that too in the early period of the net was more or less controlled. Eureka! A lot of consumers could interact with a lot of consumers but it did go through the filter of the digital high priest and some of it yet goes through that lens. It is not that the print and the net (as we saw it initially) no longer exist or are lesser important but there are more powerful phenomenon's that we have seen very recently – seems like in the last few weeks and that's the advent, rapidly adoption and growing usage of the A2A digital platforms. Scores of users embrace social networks every minute and whether that does or doesn't not bring down the need for other traditional media which includes regular websites and blogs, one thing that is for certain is that Social Media is mighty and powerful. It can make a difference to you and your brand here and now.

Mr CMO, How do you plan to reach your target audience? What's your desired response? What's your media plan? What's your media mix? Hey, What's your digital strategy? All of these now seem to be fairly simpler queries to handle than the ones that most marketing folks seem to currently dread – *What is your social media strategy? How are you leveraging social media Mr CMO? The whole world is embracing this new media but you don't have a proper plan Mr CMO?* So what's the strategy that the marketing department must have around social media? What's the magic that they need to deliver using these all powerful A2A platforms? Or must they actually be the lead department of any organization that must understand and use the social media? Is it because the word *media* follows social?

The pen is mightier than the sword. No, no! Its' the keyboard that is mightier than the sword! Did you hear someone say it is the touch-screen that is mightier than the sword! Arrghhh! Forget the pen, the stylus, the whatever and most importantly forget the sword too. But do bear in mind that the word that is being putting out now and every single second it is being put out by your customer – current or potential. And these folks are putting out lots and lots of content and they have lots and lots of places to publish their opinions and experiences that could make or break brands before you even realize it. Wouldn't it be terrific for a brand to have lots of consumers write good stories about them? But where do you find these *lots of customers*? Of course you would have a few who would for genuine reasons or for purposes of showing off write some good things about your brand? But that would happen only in case of aspirational brands or a few more. And then there are very few good or the show off category of human beings that would be saying good things. More often you find disgruntled customers who instantly take on to the new A2A platforms to vent their dissatisfaction without even knowing how to use a product or service they have procured a few minutes ago. These folks are dangerous! And beware! There are lots of them around you. Doesn't it then make sense for the customer service department to be the first to have a social media strategy? To track and bring all such cases to a happy ending so that these dissatisfied Johnny's would then speak positively about your brand, buy more of your products and more importantly bring in more customers.

Doesn't it make sense for your research department to communicate using these platforms with potential customers of a potential product they could be developing? Wouldn't such direct feedback be more valuable than any market survey? Wouldn't it make imminent sense for your production folks to communicate directly with some of your customers? To hear from them directly on what their customers think about the products and services they are putting out? Wouldn't all of this interaction excite some of your own staff? And create bonding with some percentage of your customers who could become your brand ambassadors? Wouldn't the customers to be excited to have their say?

It is apparent that leveraging social media is simply not the responsibility of only the marketing department. Today's consumer is far smarter, he is more exposed than ever before, he prefers information from peers and other users over high priests, he ain't too gullible either to buy in to smart marketing messages. This does not take away from the role of the marketing department. They very much need to be there to create constant awareness and visibility for their brands. But in my humble opinion, a social media strategy needs to be complete and holistic – it needs to allow different functions of an organization to interact with customers in an organized and structured manner. It needs to allow conversations. It needs to be designed in a manner that takes in feedback from customers at all stages in the cycle – be it pre, during or post a sale and uses it to constantly enhance the offerings. And it needs to allow your customers to interact with each other in a meaningful manner all the time. A customer engaged, happily and in a constructive manner will remain happily married to you for life.

I haven't read this book and Ashwin's promised to carry my piece unedited even if it clashed with his content. Having worked with him on multiple assignments, his views on Social Media never fail to impress me. I am sure you would find his tips on how to use this all important social platform meaningful and practical. I look forward to reading this book.

Happy Reading!!!

— **Hoshiediar Ghaswalla**
President, Cyber Media (India) Limited

INTRODUCTION

Ever wondered what the words "Social media" could mean to your business? Agreed that you are familiar with the words as you have heard it several times, but do you really know what it means? Are you sure you have a fair idea of its potential? Even if you answered any one of the above questions with a no or maybe, it is clear that you have those void spaces in your mind under the heading social media platforms. So am I going to help you with covering those knowledge gaps? Surely this book is an endeavor that I make towards it.

The buzz in town has been a lot about how each individual or brand is using this social media space to their benefit. The innovative ideas on display in this space are surely worth applauding for. The competitiveness that every brand displays in the regular market place has also being seen to be shifted to the social media space. For any business, social media platform represents a marketing opportunity that eliminates the traditional middleman and connects companies directly with customers. This is why nearly every business on the planet—from giants like Starbucks and DELL to the local ice cream shop—are exploring social media marketing initiatives. A few years ago, businesses were uncertain about social media. Now it's here to stay and brands are rapidly adopting social media marketing. Much like email and websites first empowered businesses, social media is the next marketing wave. With so much happening on this platform, it shall be foolish to keep our eyes closed to its methods and success. Very often you hear;

"Social Networking Sites Reach 60% of Global Internet Users or more"

"Twitter users welcome 2012 with 16,000 tweets-per-second, more than doubling last year's record."

"Nearly 25% of social network users say that Facebook is the site that most influences their buying decisions."

Those are just a few facts that I put together in order to lay emphasis on how much potential the world of social media network stores within itself. This is your opportunity to dig in deep and uncover those hidden potentials and to make them work for your benefit. It is important that you are aware of all the factors that are involved in social media marketing because as they say "Half knowledge is dangerous".

If you are interested to getting down straight to business and knowing how using Social Media effectively will help your brand and you grow, here is how the Social media platform will help you:

- Create a connection with your potential customers by exhibiting to them your business personality
- Create brand awareness among your target audience.
- Create customer loyalty by creating a fan base and an easy way for them to follow what you are doing
- Promote your business to many more people than you could reach by traditional advertising such as radio, TV and magazine or newspaper print
- Create a great platform to share your business values and philosophies which help will increase customer loyalty and retention

So now you know why the global giants have recognized Social

Media Marketing as a potential marketing platform, and utilized it with innovations to power their advertising campaigns.

ROLE OF SOCIAL MEDIA IN MARKETING

Social media has so much to offer that it has also now increasingly become an ingrained aspect of political campaigns, public policy, public relations, brand management and even intra company communication. Since the major task of marketing as tool used to inform consumers about your company's products, who you are and what you offer, social marketing plays an important role in marketing.

- Social media can be used to provide an identity about your brand and the products or services that you offer.
- Social media helps in creating relationships with people who might not otherwise know about the products or service or what your brand represents.
- Social media makes your brand "real" to consumers. If you want people to follow you, you need not just talk about the latest product news, but can share your personality with them.
- Social media can be used to associate your brand with your peers that may be serving the same target market.
- Social media can be used to communicate and provide the interaction that your consumers look for.

SOCIAL MEDIA MARKETING CAN'T GO UNNOTICED

Size: Facebook has over 250 million users globally. On an average, 70-100 tweets happen by the second. An average user on Facebook has 120 friends. This is the kind of enormity Social networking sites espouse and with this comes the license to communicate powerfully.

Transparency: No cheat code involved. No black hat techniques allowed. Everything that happens in the social networking landscape is fool proof. Companies cannot fake authenticity in an attempt to get more people involved. Members can choose to associate with the company or opt out. Opinions made on social networking platforms are taken seriously and the more involved the companies get, more seriously they are taken. This increases the trust that your consumers will have in your brand.

Reach: It is possible to make a mark globally and do it quickly using social networking sites.

Boost website traffic: Social media is probably the fastest and easiest means of redirecting traffic to company's website. By simply placing their website URL in your profile, you can have all your profile visitors check out their website and a percentage of traffic is sure to get converted in due course of time. This is the virtual version of "word-of mouth".

Branding: Buying a candy may have been an impulsive action all your life, but if it is discussed on a social networking site, there is a possibility that you get brand conscious even to buy a candy. Social media is a smart way to build brands. Social media platforms are known to be one of the most powerful, and among the fastest means of branding. Some of the big brands like Coke, Ford, Dell, IBM, Burger King are famous for being the early adopters of social media to endorse themselves.

Customer engagement and delight: Big brands today have understood and appreciated the fact that when it comes to marketing themselves there is nothing like engaging the customers and meanwhile delighting them as well. The underlying trick here is to focus as much as possible on building a relationship rather than just focusing on emptying their stocks by hook or crook. When the brands are here to foster their customer relationships through constantly engaging the customers, the social media platform is their best bet. Be it by regularly updating their customers or target audience with new products or services that they have to offer or hearing out on the feedback that is voiced out by the customers, customer delight is sure to come.

So whatever said and done, there is no escape from social media these days. Today, it is impossible to separate social media from the online world.

The social media conversation is no longer considered a Web 2.0 fad - it is taking place in homes, small businesses and corporate boardrooms, and extending its reach into the nonprofit, education and health sectors. It is therefore imperative to understand that today, social media has exponential potential. It is a part of an ever-growing online network of people who discuss, comment, participate, share and create. Whether you are an individual, a startup, small business or a large corporation, an online presence and an ongoing conversation with your consumers is a baseline requirement. Many brands are diverting resources and rethinking their traditional outreach strategies. And as the social media wave dissipates into the vast ocean of connected experiences, the term itself will become an entry in dictionaries and encyclopedias and we will embark on a new era of knowledge, accessibility and experiences unbound by distance, time or physical walls. It is high time that your business adopts social media and takes it seriously!

CRSO

ANALYZING THE NEED FOR SOCIAL MEDIA

The buzz bee that stung the world in the late nineties spawned into a humongous epidemic that is just too big to be ignored. Whether the world embraced social media or social media embraced the world is a question that can only be rhetorical in nature. Only through deliberate efforts and constant ignorance can one turn a blind eye to the success of social media.

The rocketing of the social media has been so instantaneous that the world is still mesmerized by its potential. The possibility of shouting out to the world without tearing down the vocal cords, connecting people who are separated by physicality and taking the freedom of expression to a whole new level are just a few endowments of the social media.

Like any logical think map, let us establish the answers to the What, Why and How of social media marketing.

• **Let's you know what your customers are saying about your brand:** Endless hours of collecting questionnaires, analyzing the results, filling in the information gap with estimations based on gut feelings are all obsolete in the wake of social media that facilitates consumer reviews and feedback in real time. Whether you would like to know if the new innovation is enough to satisfy the consumer who is in constant lookout to simplify life or if the buyer is ready to accept and pay for a slightly offbeat idea, social media offers all the answers to such inquisitions. There is no grey area left to your imagination in this process. It is just hard facts–either the consumer likes it or dislikes it. With such accurate facts, the time spent on pondering about the possible response of the audience can be metamorphosed into "Action Time" to achieve greater results. When the expectations from your product are clearly set by the end user it makes a lot more sense.

- **Helps you initiate conversations around your product and also help you get early insights while developing a new product:**

Social media gives you an incredible opportunity to listen and also initiate the conversations from your current customers and the prospective ones who openly discuss their needs, generate new product ideas and alert your issues with your existing products. Call it eavesdropping but for good! Such timely information can help in developing the product at many stages in order to gain a whole hearted acceptance from the consumer.

- **Engage relevant audience with a view to influence their purchase decision:**

No matter what business jargons are used, the only end result any marketer strives for is increase in sales and profit. One efficient way to achieve this goal is by influencing purchase decision by having a great brand recall strategy acting on the consumer's mind. Brands experiment with wide range of concepts to engage the consumer in order to stay on the top of their mind. Social media offers a plethora of opportunities to target a specific interest group on common topics in order to engage the consumer and influencing their purchase decision.

- **Developing brand image/ perception:**

"Building a brand" has been a part of the marketing textbook since a long time so has "brand perception". The newfangled idea that has tagged along over the years is creating a "Persona" for the brand. When a brand is backed by a personality and an aura the audience pick up the favorable messages that the marketer strives to convey which in turn offers higher chances to manifests into an unconscious buying decision in favor of the marketer.

- **Helps you execute effective campaigns.**

Smart brands differ in their communication strategies and targeted approach. Social media offers the stage for a "5 C campaign" to steer a brand from being 'little known' to 'popular'. The 5 C's signify:

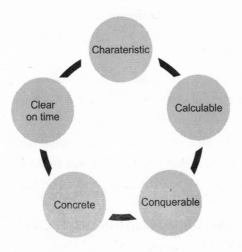

Characteristic: A communication strategy that highlights the characteristic of your product and builds to the persona can be developed on the social media platform. This will help the audience relate better to the brand.

Calculable: The result of any campaign determines its success and therefore need to be calculable. A vague idea about the possible effectiveness of a campaign not backed by any hard facts is just futile. Social media offers instant data of the success of the campaign backed by numerical data and comments.

Concrete: Building castles in the air and painting highly optimistic pictures are easy paces towards being carried away from reality. But when reality hits, it hits hard. The goal therefore needs to be a concrete and realistic idea that can be derived out of historical figures in order to stick the feet on to the ground. Social media thus provides an insight into the results of previous campaigns and their effectiveness in order to determine concrete plans.

Conquerable: Of what use is a fancy goal setting list, if it is not attainable? Once the ideas are in place they need to be tested on their do-ability factor. Social media offers to determine the conquerable factor of the goals, set more and even higher achievable goals for the campaign.

Clear on time: Any good goal needs to be time bound in order to reap benefits at the desired time and situation. Without a time plan, the seemingly ever continuing efforts will eventually drain out all the energy and patience with little or no effect. Since social media responses are instantaneous the time that one needs to wait for to know the results is largely reduced and can be defined depending on the target audience.

WHY SHOULD AN ORGANIZATION GO SOCIAL?

Organization should go social mainly to benefit from the integration of the "Wonder C's" that the social media beautifully weaves into itself.

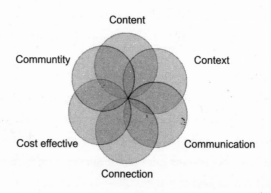

Content: Social Media gives organizations an opportunity to promote their content. This content could be in the form of case-studies, whitepapers, articles or simply a brief on product features In the process it will also be able to identify the relevant target audience that it needs to focus on.

Communication: Communication plays a great role in marketing. The need to continuously communicate with the end user in order to keep them informed and get feedback is the backbone of any good campaign. Social media also offers opportunities to educate the relevant audience about the organization's offering in order to help the customers realize their need for the product. By such efforts the needs that even the customer is unaware of can be discovered and fulfilled.

Cost effective: Time is money in the true sense in the context of social media. Apart from time, the investment required is bare minimum. This is one of the factor that set social media apart from any other media available for communication. Only when you make a conscious investment in enhancing any aspect does the money factor come into picture.

Connection: Instead of just being a one way communication medium, social media connects the marketer and audience like never before. The marketers now "listen" to the consumer instead of just rubbing their promotion material against the audience. This way the prospective customer is aware of the USP's of the business without it being forced on them.

Community: Creating communities around a particular product not only increases brand loyalty but also is a great way to analyze every campaign in order to determine its success and your ROI . (ROI refers to "Return on Investment") Communities help you assess the reach of every campaign. You can discover how many people viewed it, watched the video about your product, claimed a coupon to avail discounts on near-by outlets, and finally, how many people bought it. This way, communities on Social Media help you precisely judge how much sale was made due to a marketing campaign.

HOW WILL SOCIAL MEDIA HELP ME ACHIEVE MY MARKETING GOALS FASTER?
Chance on grabbing many eyeballs with one click

"One in every 9 people on the planet is on Facebook"

"People spend 700 billion minutes per month on Social Media"

"If Facebook were a country, it would be the world's third largest country (after China and India) and 2 times the size of US population.

With such facts glaring at us in the face could we risk not hopping into the band wagon of social media marketers? The vast spread offered by Social Media Marketing is simply phenomenal and wipes out any boundaries.

Focusing on the niche audience

When focused attention is given to the right audience the results are much more fruitful than any form of expensive general communication where you are not sure of who is listening to you. Such distinct communication is a blessing offered by the social media platform which segregates the audience for you.

Finding and activating niche brand ambassadors

These are the individuals who influence many people's decision due to their strong views and opinions about products in a certain category. Finding such brand ambassadors and getting them to talk about you is a stepping stone to success for the marketer.

The opportunity to go viral

Social media is like word of mouth on steroids. When the brand catches the attention of the social media space, it is tried, tested and spoken about by many to many. This provides a great opportunity for the brands to spread positive words.

A FEW POINTS TO KEEP IN MIND BEFORE DECIDING TO INDULGE IN SOCIAL MEDIA

Just as every medicine can't be prescribed to all, social media may not always be an answer for all the establishments. In order to be sure if social media is right for you, check a few points before you take a head long plunge into the world of social media hoping for miracles to happen.

The signs that social networking might not be a good fit for your priorities

You're still trying to get a hold on your basic software infrastructure. The market place out there provides for a number of software solutions that can enhance your organization's effectiveness and efficiency. Almost all organizations will get more 'bang for their buck' by ensuring that they are using efficient software solutions specially designed to suit their needs like customer relationship management, inventory checks, online transaction gateways etc. Once these fundamentals are in order, it makes more sense to turn your attention to experimental areas like social networking.

However if you're looking for an easy way to build a simple Web site and your audience overlaps substantially with the younger and more tech-savvy audiences likely to be using MySpace or Facebook, it's worth considering using social networking tools to create a Web presence by integrating the social media platforms into your website to create a more rounded platform.

Your target audience may not be as tech savvy as you think they are

Social networking is an answer to those businesses that wish to reach-out or work with community members on Facebook or MySpace. For this type of audience rather than expecting them to join you on a new site it becomes necessary to find ways to interact with them using the existing platform.

Even though the older audience is testing the waters in the social media world and trying to find a foot hold, the cyber space is dominated by the young and tech-savvy audience. So a general communication on any platform does not provide an answer. You should go about learning what sites your target audiences are using. There's no better way than asking them, either through a survey or informal one-on-one interviews.

You are short of time and patience to nurture it before it bears fruits

Online communities aren't self-maintaining. They need you to promote them, cultivate them, and give them directions. If your network blossoms, you may be able to step back and watch your users produce and share content. But getting to that point takes a lot of time and effort.

What's more, this work is not likely to yield immediate, measurable, bottom-line returns on your time invested. There are some examples of organizations attracting large numbers of supporters to sign a petition or to become "friends" within a social networking site. This can be helpful in marketing your organization, but it's often hard to convert these online associations into more traditional supporters. But keep in mind that there's no guarantee.

You're not willing to deal with technologies that don't work as well as they could

What worked today may not work tomorrow. What worked for others may not work for you. This being very relevant on the technology front, an organization needs to be prepared to constantly work on it in order to figure out how things should be. If your organization decides to invest in social networking, you'll need a reliable consultant or a staff member who is willing to experiment, figure out how to get stuff working, and approach these tools with a sense of adventure. They'll need patience to deal with platforms that don't necessary work as well as they could, or even as well as advertised.

You're not ready to invest in gaining a real understanding of the medium

If you think that rubbing any kind of promotional material against the audience will be more than enough, think again! Such an attitude could do you more harm than good. In order to have success with social networking, it's critical that you understand the culture of the communities you're joining. Typical social networking site users expect a collaborative, open approach. Anything that seems like a hard sell or like it was put together by a committee will be ignored, or, worse, ridiculed.

You want clear editorial control over your brand and message

Once you are out there in the social space you have little or no control over the conversations that happen. If you are not willing to stick around and turn everything that comes your way to your advantage social media may not be right for you.

Only when you are sure that you would not have any of the above pitfalls you need to venture out into the world of social media to achieve your purpose.

TOP 10 QUESTIONS TO ANSWER BEFORE YOU GO 'SOCIAL'

Whether you want to test the waters at social media through a specific social channel and customer segment or there's a strategic effort at implementing a social business strategy, working through a questionnaire can be very useful for effective planning.

While every company and customer base is unique, questions need to be asked as they provide a valuable insight into your business state of social media marketing readiness as well as provoking new thoughts and direction. The more informed you are about planning for the social web, the more successful you will be.

Here are 10 questions worth considering in order to put yourself in the right perspective:

1. Do you know what your customers' preferences for social, content, discovery, consumption, and sharing are?
2. Are your goals well defined?
3. What will be the factors that you will consider in order to measure success of your social media experiment? What key performance indicators (KPI) are most relevant for your goals?
4. What processes will you need to implement to ensure proper tagging of social content and coordination with the technology department for reporting?
5. Do you have a monitoring application in place in order to monitor the social space?
6. Are there unsponsored social media accounts operating on behalf of the brand?
7. Is a dashboard and campaign management tool in place for social media management, content promotion, and measurement?
8. How will corporate social media marketing efforts coordinate with other SEO(Search Engine Optimization), content marketing, and external communications?
9. Do you have enough people to create content, develop a network, promote your business, monitor and analyze the activity?
10. Does it make sense for the business to scale social media participation to facilitate external social media communications?

Now that we have explored all the spheres of social media marketing, we could move on to get our basics right.

CRXEO

Step 2

GETTING THE BASICS RIGHT

Once the decision to leverage social media has been taken, it is of utmost importance to champion the nitty-gritty of social media.

To get started in Social Media, you must consider and plan for the following:

Come up with interesting content that people would love to share: If your content is all about standard marketing lines and tactics, why would your audience want to share it among their network? They surely do not want to be your ambassador by risking their reputation in the society. In this light, it is very important to keep in mind that your audience will be linked to your content in the public eye. When interesting content is drafted, your existing audience shall help you grab many more eyeballs while aggrandizing their own social image.

Simplify Sharing: Now that the audience like your content—the simpler it is to share, the more likely they are to do so. It just takes a moment for the mind to like the content and generate a need to tell others about it. In that moment if any such sharing medium is available in sight, the mind immediately takes advantage of the same and shares the content with its peers. The more time that one needs to search of ways to share the content, the more will be the decline in interest to share it. Hence it gets really important to make sure the share tab is located within the viewing range for the eye to pick up the signal as the mind decides it wants to share the content. The lesser the delay, the better!

Add the extra zing by rewarding engagement: Reward makes everything sweeter and more appealing too. When you start reciprocating people's conversations about your brand with small gestures, they know how much they mean to you. The fact that they feel important will encourage them to take their engagements further. There could be numerous discussions, polls, blogs and comments about your brand. These could prove of great help to your brand if thoroughly monitored and answered to wherever necessary. It thus becomes very crucial to encourage such engagements at all times. So, reward more to be rewarded back.

Share wherever possible: Explore all the possible channels that you could use to get your message out loud and clear. Whatever suits your target audience is the right way for you to take be it tweeting, digging or using RSS feed. There can be no assumptions made when deciding on what your target audience could possibly be using as their window to the world. Determining the sites they prefer could be done by surveys and also by integrating various "know your customer" form filling within your business. So, speak in their language when you need them to understand.

Encourage dialects to be added to your language: Allow people to find your content and put it in their own dialect. The more the adaptation from your original content, the better reach you are gifted with. After a certain point every business will find it difficult to expand their horizon in order to find newer sets of audience for their content. This could be due to many factors like encourage people to sing your song in their voice to their people.

After gaining knowledge about what is to be done in order to use the space successfully, it becomes important to lay down guidelines, policies and procedures in order to avoid any unfair deviations.

From an organization point of view, Social Media marketing cannot be a one-man show. It needs to be supported by a number of individuals within the organization as well as outside the organization. With so many people involved, it becomes necessary to have policies and procedures that people can adhere to.

SOCIAL MEDIA POLICIES

An ideal Social Media policy document needs to lay down the following:

1. Guidelines on how to handle the issue of granting employees the right to access any form of Social Media within the organization or outside.
2. Guidelines on the required level of employment disclosure.
3. Guidelines to prohibit any kind of deformation activity by the employees over Social Media that might be harmful for the business in any way.
4. Guidelines on how to go about the Social media confidentiality and Non disclosure policies that needs to be followed in order to prevent any information leaks from within the organization.
5. Guidelines clearly demarcating official and personal communication so that further discrepancies don't arise.
6. Guidelines defining digital citizenship of an employee and the freedom allowed to them in the view of preventing any undue situations that might arise in the future.
7. Policies regarding the various training programs planned with the view to make the organization better adaptable to social media.
8. Guidelines to regulate the activities of contractors, vendors or any

other external parties to the organization over social media so as to keep a check that the organization is not being pulled into any unfavorable situations due to such associations.

Every single detail that can be planned for needs to be clearly laid out for the benefit or the business along with the other parties involved with the business. This shall ensure that there is no gap for hazy situations where one is left not knowing how to react to it.

INVESTMENT REQUIRED FOR A SUCCESSFUL SOCIAL MEDIA CAMPAIGN

With so much in store, Social media has become every smart businesses trumpet that they blow hard to let the world know more about them. With such loud trumpets blowing from all the directions the social media has become just as competitive to attract attention as it is in the market place. Just as every marketer fights it out to differentiate themselves in the market place every business on social media platform strives to stand out from the rest of the crowd.

With differentiation being on every business's agenda only some businesses manage to truly individualize themselves by putting in the extra effort required. Instead of just trying out the social media space as a "Nothing to lose" option, these businesses are willing to put in their bets in order to reap the benefits. They don't shy away from putting in their investments for the social space in the form of time, human resources and advertisements on a number of popular sites. This distinct attitude and spirit sets them apart from the rest.

When such success stories portray the need to solicit efforts along with investments it gets hard to ignore. Imagine time as water for the social media plant, human resources as air and the expenditure of advertising on popular sites like Facebook, Google's contextual ads etc. as the manure to boost its growth. It thus becomes evident that they are aids that shall help the plant blossom and yield desired results.

Now that we have already spoken about what a smart business does to make its mark, it also becomes important to know how a social media marketer differentiates himself from the traditional marketer.

1. The old school marketer's never really realized the importance of building conversations around their brand and what it could do to the brand image. The new trend revolves exclusively around getting people to talk and talk about the brand with the view to go viral and to let the brand reach a larger audience.

2. After the industrial revolution brought in the automation bug into the world, people began adapting this school of thought in every phase of life. Traditional marketers were no exception. They firmly began to believe in automating their response in order to avoid wasting their time or putting in any efforts in personalizing the response. However, the new breed of marketers begs to differ from this school of thought. They believe in personalizing the interactions in order to develop a genuine relationship with the customer. Such attention to details makes the communication more effective with hints of personal touches all the way.

3. Sending in standard forms of communication into the large space of all media is now obsolete. Same is true for just bombarding the audience with typical marketing material without considering the differences that lie in each target group or listening to them. The game in the past was all about numbers and nothing else mattered as much. But the new age thinkers turned around this attitude by introducing the need to listen to the target audience before deciding on what should be done in order to grab their attention. With ears wide open their communication became more targeted and specific instead of shouting out into void space and hoping for some response. This way it has become more economical in term of time, money and effort.

4. With traditional marketers just wanting to appease customers by hook or crook, began an era of mass appeal offers and meager discounts. The game was never about benefiting the customer or

finding solutions to their concerns. With the decline of this era began a new one that was customer centric. It was all about creating value for the customer and building a relationship of trust with them. This trust based relationship metamorphosed into customer loyalty which in turn rewarded the marketer.

5. Traditional marketers based their major decisions on numbers and were impatient in a way. They needed numbers to speak the language of success for them almost immediately after they put in any form of efforts. They believed the world is just black and white. Either a particular group is worth the investment or it is not based on its first responses to the marketer's efforts.

   When such quick decisions took form, there was no time to nurture relationships. This was turned around by the new age marketers who believed in investing long term in any good marketing strategy and nurturing it in order to reap its benefits. Patience and perseverance defined their approach which was more rewarding than ever.

   Now that all the basics needed have been touched upon, it becomes necessary to clearly define who the brand is and what its needs are.

CR80

INTROSPECT: IDENTIFY YOUR STRENGTHS

A kid's performance is analyzed through exams in school and success of a marketing effort undertaken is analyzed using the sales figures. The need to convert all information into solid figures stems from the fact that figures make it easier to analyze performance. The obsession with numbers is because they present the scenario in black and white to facilitate better analysis. With the same rule applying to the social media space it becomes important that every brand determines the canopy of its existing reach in the social media in order to clearly define the areas that need to be focused on.

After understanding the need to analyze the brand's reach, now is the time to figure out how strong your brand or product (or the segment you are targeting), is online. You could start with analyzing your current clout on social media, who are the influencers in your brand category and what are they saying about you.

In an era of quick help and information, after the need is identified, the solution is not too far away. Hence, begin with identifying how you or your brand is perceived online. Below are a few ways to determine your clout on social media.

Klout   A brands clout on social media is steered by the 'influence' it has on the online users. An online tool - Klout- helps you measure the amount of influence you could have on social media users. By acquiring data based on the account activities over networks like Facebook, Twitter, LinkedIn and Foursquare it offers a measure of your influence on a scale of 1 to 100. It sheds light on how many people you influence (true reach), how much you influence them (amplification), and how influential they are (network score), and assigns a score from 1 to 100.

TwentyFeet   Being able to get access to all the social engagement data that you need using only one tool can truly be a delight. TwentyFeet is one such data consolidator tool that integrates all your social media. It consolidates data from Twitter, Facebook, bit.ly, YouTube, Google Analytics, MySpace, FriendFeed, and RSS feeds and presents you with an easy to use and understand analysis in one place. When something big is happening out there, with TwentyFeet you shall not miss it.

PeerIndex   The PeerIndex algorithm measures the speed at which content travel happens along with the volume of content shared. When any content is re-tweeted or is commented on, it increases the Peerindex score. It measures the acceptability factor for any content and thus can help you while designing your content.

Empire Avenue   Empire Avenue is essentially a social networking game that allows you to connect with individuals based on "value relationships" — the much closer relationships than just having someone follow you on Twitter or "Like" you on Facebook. The platform can bring together highly engaged individuals around the world across a wide variety of interests. It enables you to get in front of new audience and connect with relevant customers.(Website is www.empireavenue.com)

Sprout Social   Sprout Social integrates the various social media platforms like Twitter, Facebook Fan Pages, LinkedIn, Foursquare, Gowalla, and other networks with the motive to enable the business to engage in consumer discussions around their brands and products. In addition to communication tools, Sprout Social helps to manage contacts, provides competitive insights and also helps to generate leads. (Website www.sproutsocial.com)

Crowdbooster   Crowdbooster provides social media popularity measurement tools along with recommendations to help your business build a strong social media presence. It evaluates your social media strategy based on the factors like total reach, engagement and more. (Website www.crowdbooster.com)

Twylah   Twylah believes in the idea that context is just as important as the data itself. It is a tool that helps in building a body around a skeletal content. It brings in the contextual relevance into play in order to boost the contents value. It showcases your tweets in a more complete narrative story and aids in making the content far more interesting than just a regular tweet. (Website www.twylah.com)

My Web Career   My Web Career unravels the spread of your social media presence and also determines the digital footprint that you leave behind. It provides a complete picture of how successful you are on the social media platform. It could be very useful when you are looking for a rounded picture in order to draw inferences and layout strategies based on them. (Website www.mywebcareer.com)

Appinions   Opinions of users are the most valuable resources to tap into for any brand. Appinion understands this like nobody else. It is a tool that helps to voice out opinions of millions of user on web spaces like blogs, Twitter, Facebook, forums, newspaper and magazine articles. It is an opinion-powered platform that makes it easy to identify, analyze, monitor and engage with influencers. It not only focuses on the influencers creating content, but on the influencers attracting the most attention. (Website www.appinions.com) With so many options within reach you could easily wander around baffled by them. Deciding which site makes more sense to you and is apt for your needs can be a 'Herculean' task.

However, I recommend you start with www.klout.com and www. socialmention.com to judge your brands perception and image on social media. These website help you discover the product/service/brands existing influence, amplification, network, strength, true reach, passion, sentiment, Top keywords, and top hash tags, on Social Media.

Before jumping on to know-how to achieve all this, it will make a lot more sense for us to discuss what meaning each of the term listed above carry in the context of social media.

INFLUENCE

Influence can be defined as an ability to drive action. It is a measure of how much weight a brand's value carries in the decision making process of individuals. The higher the number of people to whom a brand matters, the higher will be its score of influential capability. It is definitely not something that is earned in a day or two. It is the constant engagement that a brand puts that earns it the influencing power over time. With the right modus, the influence can be made to branch out wide as well as grow stronger. The stronger the influence network that a brand is able to build; the better it will be for the brand presence. Websites like Klout measure the influence foothold of a brand by measuring factors like how many people does the brand hold an influence on, how much of an influence does it have and how influential are they influenced by the brand.

AMPLIFICATION

To amplify means to make larger, greater or stronger. This is one such feature that social media has to offer that no medium so far has been able to deliver with such great results. Social media provides a profound advantage of facilitating businesses to tap into networks within their network.In that way not only do you have a network, but every node in your network has a network of its own that increases the very important influencing power of the brand. Thus social media aid in intensifying the message that a brand wishes to convey and there by nourishes its prosperity. Strategically using these networks by gathering and sharing relevant content can position a brand as an industry thought leader. There are many websites that help to calibrate the amount of amplification effect that each brand can take benefit of with its present network.

NETWORK

As already put forth social media space offers an incredible reach amidst your target audience. The wider and stronger the social web presence is, the more attention your brand shall call for. The magic concoction that social media has managed to latch on so beautifully is the fact that after a point in time the social web presence manages to grow virally without any extra effort or expenditure. Every time a user decides to share your content across his network you are building a new network for your brand. Thus, offering the most effective platform in terms of the return of investment calculation.

STRENGTH

As a brand grows into an influential brand there are various benefits that come with it. One of the many blessings that come along is the power of strength and a considerable amount of dominance. With the brand growing stronger every minute, it will eventually attain the status of the industry thought-leader. It will grow to the extent wherein dominance over the other players in the space will be its most evident outcome. With such a reach and dominance it shall there forth influence the decisions of the other brands either as a conscious strategy or an indirect effect of its business decisions.

TRUE REACH

True reach can be defined as the actual number of people who are influenced by you and your presence on the social media platform. In order to arrive at the true reach numbers it becomes important to filter out spams and bots thus focusing on the people who are actually influenced by the brand. Websites like Klout do promise to churn out the true reach number after taking into account such factors of spam and bots. Therefore obtaining the right picture before jumping into any sort of conclusion has become easier than ever before thus aiding in making the right decisions at the right time.

PASSION

Tools like Klout and Socialmention.com help to identify the passion that the target audience shares for the brand. It helps to know how much love for the brand its followers possess and the kind of connect they feel with the brand. This helps to build the brand image, thereby increasing the bond of the brand among its target audience.

SENTIMENT

Only if the end user is able to catch on and connect to the brand sentiment conveyed will he be influenced to favor the brand and its values. If the correct sentiment doesn't come across or the people are unable to decipher it, it becomes a flaw in the marketing strategy of the brand. With the view to overcome such flaws it becomes necessary for the brand to be able to truly pin point the kind of sentiment that is communicated by the brand and how it is perceived by the end user. With such kind of info generation across websites, it becomes simpler to be able to generate the right kind of campaign with the view to get the right brand message through to the target audience.

TOP KEYWORDS

Any content that is posted on the social media wall is done with the view of attracting attention towards a brand. In order to be discovered by the customer in need it becomes essential to know the top keywords that the customer is likely to search for. The more keywords are embedded in your content, more will be the chances for the customer with a need to find you. This is the most effective form of target marketing and has a high success rate due to the fact that it is the customer who comes in search of a solution rather than you chasing them. And so being able to get data on the top keywords used to search a particular kind of content and including them in your content will boost your presence on the social media by making your brand more searchable.

TOP HASH TAGS

Hash tags characteristically contain the pound sign (#) is at the crux. Putting symbols in front of words for naming purposes isn't a new concept. The '@' sign has been at the center of email universe for decades now. Many brands are now in the process of using hash tags in order to leverage their presence on the social media network. Hash tags are social media conversation for a particular group and they are one way to share your ideas, conversations and content beyond your loyal group of immediate followers on social media networks. So how do you find these groups and more importantly, how do you find the groups that are most likely to be interested in what you have to share? If you just only make up a hash tag, it does not guarantee any attention grabbing. So it becomes essential to be aware of the top hash tags that could be used to gather attention. This essential step could be achieved with the help of websites like Klout and social mention that help to identify the various trends prevailing in the world of social media.

The bottom line for this chapter will be that you need to target on improving your influence online. Increase in influence could be the result of improving amplification, network, strength, true reach, passion, sentiment, top keywords and top hash tags as discussed above which in turn can be the result of engagement, likes and shares on the social media platform. The world of social media is interconnected like a web indeed!

CRSO

PRE-CAMPAIGN BRAINSTORMING

The truth of the universe remains that whenever we meet the need, we can be assured to meet the solution sooner or later depending on the insistence of the need. For this to hold well, context doesn't really play a very ponderous part. Now that your need for social media marketing is established along with the imperative knowledge of where you currently stand, brainstorming session is inevitably the next step to take.

While planning a social media strategy, every effort aimed at achieving greater clarity and focus sweetens the deal. The tiniest of the details if paid attention to, can translate into greater return on investment. After understanding the importance of these sessions for the success of your campaign, let us dig in further.

It doesn't really make a difference if you are planning a branding initiative or a thought leadership program. Whether you are just trying to generate leads or build a social web presence. Whatever you choose to term it at the end of the day what we are really looking at is to reach out to our target audience out there. Before we take it any further, since we are so keen on getting the target audience to be interested in us maybe it is time we start calling them interest groups!

Now that we realize how important these interest groups are to us, let us try to determine who they really are. Instead of a vague idea about the possible audience to your brand, a concrete understanding shall do a lot more good. As a starting point to this discovery, I would suggest you to write down the description of your perfect audience. Define your customers or prospective ones as narrowly as possible. Try determining their age groups and gender. Are they married, engaged or single? Where do they live and what are their interests? What is the kind of jobs they hold and where do they work? What is it that they are interested to talk about? What would their hobbies be? You may feel that you really don't need answers to some of the above questions but I suggest you still find them. Answering those questions will enable you to draw a clearer picture of who you customer is and who you want him to be (if that is ever possible). While trying to answer these questions you may be also led to some more questions that could be more relevant to your specific interest group.

Once you have defined who belong to your interest group, start looking out for them. Find them on the social networks. Get to know where they huddle up and share their interests. Social networking platforms themselves offer solutions to know more about interest groups and their online behaviors. You could use Facebook's advertising platform to see exactly how many people fit the bill that you have just jotted down. If you are in the B2Bspace (Business to business model) you could use platforms like LinkedIn to filter your searches by job titles or industry. Since you have also defined their interest you could search Twitter and Facebook using these filter and locate your interest group. If your interest group says anything like young, happening or social, look no further than popular online hangouts. The online hangouts can be ibibo, Facebook, Twitter, blog, etc. these are places where you can catch your interest group in action.

After knowing who your interest groups are and where to find them, the money question comes into picture. You will need to figure out a list of places in your marketing budget where you are spending too much money by targeting your efforts towards a wider audience. Generalized marketing efforts are an easy way to market your brand but the return on investment figures are much lower than what they could be in targeted marketing. It is therefore important that we determine how you could reallocate your marketing budget in order to make more space for targeted marketing campaigns using social networks. This permutation will help you to derive a more efficient marketing campaign for your brand without being heavy on the pockets.

Let us now answer the next logical question- How do you find out how many of your target interest group are on social platform, or let's say-Facebook, without paying a dime?

As pointed out in chapter 2 Facebook boast of over 900 million users-enough to qualify as the third largest nation in the world if it were a nation. What better place to start to discover the "Number" of people around who fall under your interest group.

While Facebook ads aren't free, of course, it provides a self serve ad platform that helps an advertiser easily research exactly how many people on Facebook fit into whatever targeting criteria he desires. This platform could be used by you to find your interest group among hundreds of millions of people by simply selecting the exact attributes you were looking for in your interest group.

Before we jump on to know all that is in store for targeting, let's just cover how to initiate the search on Facebook:

On the Facebook login page you will be able to find Advertising on the bottom of the page.

You could click on create an ad

Provide in some details about the ad you would like to create (come up with some random details if you are just here to explore the tool).

Once redirected to Targeting section you will be able to type in the criteria and find the reach that you could possible get using Facebook alone. Below attached are a few screenshots of various targeting criteria available for your research.

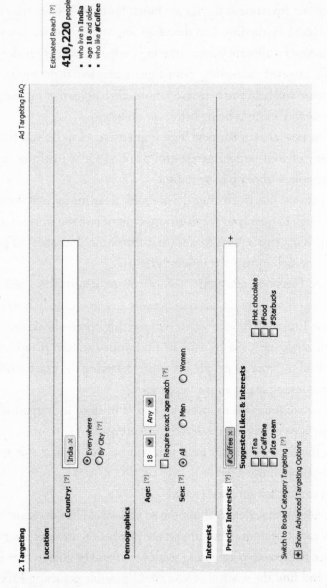

The 'interests' field could be switched into a broad category that will provide you with many more options to search.

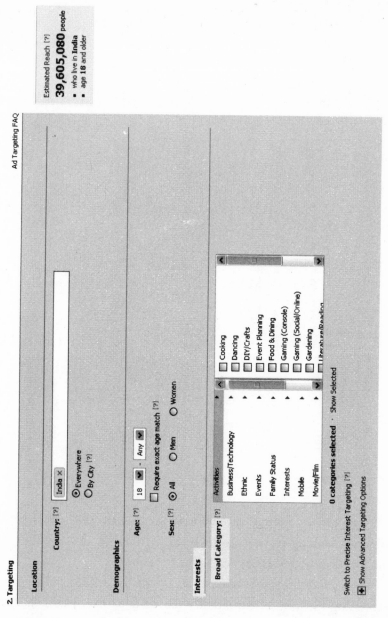

Facebook also allows you to search by criteria's like relationship status, languages, education, or even workplaces. This can be found under Advanced Targeting Options.

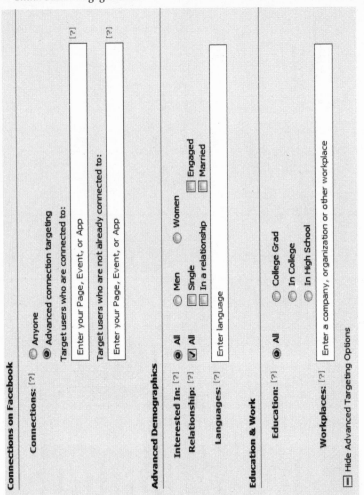

The interest groups can be found on all platforms. Every brand which is looking to tap into its interest group on this social media platform has something stored for it. For example:

In a Hotel industry context, social media is filled with people expressing the kind of cuisine they like or don't like, places they are regular to and the reasons to it, etc. Every bit of information that a hotelier looks for is just out there for them to pick up.

In the telecom industry context, social media finds people who are openly expressing their discontent with a particular service provider. Getting to know such information about their own brand or the competitor's brand straight from the horse's mouth is a boon to any marketer.

In the writer's world, knowing how many people like what you have to say and what they think you could do better is a gift of improvement given by the social media.

Knowing what social media could mean to all, irrespective of the industry is enlightening. Would you not like to know how the others have put targeting into use? Sure you do. Here are some examples of how target marketing has been used for benefit.

1. A coffee shop targeted Twitter users who check in to coffee shops on Foursquare more than five times a week within 1 km of its location.
2. A fitness club built a community site specifically for members who are athletes to exchange tips with one another.
3. An independent Samsung retailer targeted smart phone users in the 5 km radius of where it is located.

There could be instances where you are not really happy with where you are looking for your interest groups. You could feel like you are not covering the place enough to reach all your interest groups. To help you clarify such doubts and understand how your target audience uses social media you could use the following services:

Strategic Oxygen   A company that is dedicated to offer planning tools for integrated marketing is aptly called Strategic Oxygen. The data it provides could be used to effectively target buyers for any brand's products or services.

globalwebindex.net   If understanding your interest groups online behavior is what you are looking for, look no further. globalwebindex.net is a detailed market research covering consumer internet behavior, motivations and attitudes of social media users.

pewinternet.org   If you want to go that extra mile to get your facts well, pewinternet.org could provide you with research data needed.

Radian6 tools   If you don't mind spending some money to get the real scoop from real-time customer conversations Radian6 is the tool for you. It is listening tool to figure out your interest groups online likes and dislikes. It is a bit expensive ($8000) but is surely a more effective tool than Socialmention. It is being used by big guys like Dell, Microsoft, Pepsi, Samsung, Volkswagen, ICICI bank etc.

PERSONIFYING YOUR BRAND

Having initiated the journey into fine tuning marketing efforts in the targeted marketing space, let us now take it a step further. If merely segregating your interest group from the rest could give you so much, imagine what could be achieved if your brand is empowered to do all the talking by it. What if you could personify your brand and get the right messages across to your interest groups. I speak of this personification because according to many industry experts identity marketing is a well rounded smooth marketing strategy that can manifest a brand from being just another one on the list to a powerful brand.

Identity marketing can be seen as an aftermath of evolutionary brawl that every brand indulged in to make sure it could individualize itself from the rest. It has been a survival strategy to some and a step up strategy for the others. Whatever category it is classified under, it is definitely a rage in the marketing world today.

To create that compelling identity for your brand, start with setting the objectives along with jotting down the personality traits that could describe your brand. Think of traits that are characteristic to your brand. Refer to the data about your interest group that you previously spelled out, for clues. Harmonize on traits that fit in perfectly in describing both your brand as well as your interest group.

Now is the time to fit in the pieces to reveal the picture. It is important that you connect the traits into forming a complete brand personality. The brand personality needs to be empowered enough to converse that talk to the interest group at both conscious as well as sub-conscious levels. If a strong personality is successfully created, it works its magic even without the person himself realizing or being able to reason out his liking towards a particular brand.

After all the ground work on what a brand personality should ideally be, let us establish how it could be achieved. You could start with expressing your brand personality traits in terms of archetypes. An archetype is defined as a perfect or typical specimen to any character. You should ideally derive these archetypes from your brands USP (Unique Selling Point). Since the idea here is to indirectly convey the brands differentiation point, a lot of care needs to be taken while deciding on the archetypes. If an archetype that is not well defined or that does not adhere to the brand values is chosen, it could pose a threat of misinformed audience. In order to get the right messages across, you could use a small collection of archetypes as well.

Once the archetype is determined, you will need to establish the correct physical evidences to reinforce the desired message. Physical evidence works at directing untold messages through look and feel to the brain, and influences brand perception. It becomes important to get the visual cues right that could speak the essence of the brand personality. These will become invaluable as you develop your brand personality and supporting design elements.

In the entire process of coming up with the correct brand personality you will need to keep in mind the following five points:

Take the honest way: Your brand is what it is. Any questionable claims built around your brand shall only lead to loss of credibility in the long run. People respect brands that are honest and ethical. Earn that adoration and you are right on track.

Consistency is the key: Your brands marketing efforts over the social media should not be a combination of downpour and drought. It should be like a well watered garden hustling with life. Consistent efforts will succeed in keeping the social media audience engaged throughout and will add to the brand perception.

Relevance is very relevant: It is necessary that your brand engages in relevant conversation rather than in every other conversation on social media. This shall add to the focus and project your brand as a no nonsense brand.

Know your platform well: Different platforms on social media address different needs and audience. It is therefore necessary that you know and understand the platforms audience well in order to ensure effective marketing campaign.

Keep change constant: In this dynamic world of social media adapting to change is a key to survival. Be prepared for it!

After knowing what your brand personality should be like, let us look at how you could achieve a high brand recall for that personality.

- Let the pixels do the talking for your brand: A picture can speak a thousand words. Use more visually attractive content in your social media posts in order to be remembered better.
- Voice your opinion: Speak up about what you feel about topics relevant to your brand directly or indirectly. This shall add to your brands personality.
- Play those videos: What a picture or text misses, a video captures perfectly. It grabs the necessary attention and also works on content retention and recall like no other. Use it in your engagements wherever possible.
- Let the creative juices flow: When the content echoes creativity, it is admired by the audience. This admiration manifests into a greater attention and brand recall. This is because the mind registers

the content that it finds interesting for a longer period of time in comparison to any regular content.

As discussed earlier, it is of utmost importance that any social media marketing effort needs to have clearly defined objectives in order to ensure that you are on the desired path.

How have you been tracking your progress in order to adjust your objectives? What should you look out for?

In order to understand your brands image better, you could integrate tools into your study in order to look out for the following factors:

Volumes: Like any good measure, a study on the volume attracted by your brand's marketing effort will help analyze your interest group's behavior towards various stimuli. This way you could study what are the high yielding strategies and use them in your efforts more often. So keep an eye on those numbers

Conversations about your brand: Monitor the conversations about your brand to know what people think of you and how you could better your brand perception. It will give you an insight into the other side of your social media image.

Your social media dominance: When two brands are doing the exact same business and using the same media for communication, in an idealistic world we would expect the same output as well. However in this less than perfect world, brands cash in on doing minute things right in order to set them apart. Try evaluating your brands efforts in light of your competitor's effort to get an idea of how they differ and how you could better yours.

Audience engagement: When a brand communicates and receives response from the audience, it is being heard and understood. However, if this engagement is temporary or a one-time thing it will yield no benefits. So there is a need to make sure you engage your audience over longer stretches of time and also have numbers backing it.

Based on your progress as determined by the above methods, you could now look at setting those social media objectives for your brand. Please note that the list could be exhaustive. Just to give you an idea I shall try listing the most common social media objectives. You could customize it according to your brands needs.

Generic goals	Outcome-based goals
Increasing the site traffic	• Increase the number of back links to the site. • Increase the number of hits to the site by 30%
Serve the customer well	• Increase customer satisfaction by responding to their queries and complaints efficiently. • Decrease the time taken to respond to the customers concerns and achieve greater turnaround rate.
Keep potential customers closer	• Create communities around your brand and engage in discussions and information sharing. • Increase the ROI for a marketing campaign by 25% but targeting the efforts.
Get thought leaders to talk about you	• Increase brand popularity by getting the thought leaders of the industry to share their opinion about your brand.
Understand your brands perception	• Improve brand perception by knowing what people think of you and making special efforts to better your best.
Differentiate from the rest	• Introduce new initiatives to improve sales by 30% year on. • Exhibit greater brand presence by being creative at every stage.
Build buzz around the product	• Increase share of voice to 50+ percent during 30 days preceding new product launch • Extend conversation reach to exceed internal benchmarks by 20% within 60days of product launch

Grow emerging markets	• Increase traffic to new product pages from one region by 35% during one year • Build audience engagement with target audience to 40% in a year
Increase revenue	• Generate 100 qualified leads per social media campaign within 90 days of product launch • Achieve sales of Rs.1,00,000 within 12 months of new product launch through social media engagement

GETTING THE WEBSITE READY

Now that the objective and the milestones are set, let us do a check. Is your website ready to take a plunge into the social media world? Does your website have in hand all that is necessary for the social media stage? Here is a checklist to help you answer these questions and bring in more clarity.

1. Does your website have any email listing technology embedded to it?
2. Is your website user-friendly? Does it eliminate the need for technical knowledge to add any content to your site?
3. Is your content informative to the customer? If yes, is it informative enough?
4. Does your website facilitate building of conversations around your product?
5. Does your website favor sharing among the social media world using re-posts, re-tweets, etc.?
6. Is your website open source so that you don't miss out on access to inexpensive developers and important updates?
7. Does your website ask and record enough feedback at all stages from the user?
8. Are there enough pages linked to your website that could speak more about your brand?
9. Does your website offer various ways to subscribe for updates using RSS feeds, newsletters etc.
10. Does your site offer ease of navigation along with built in search

functions to enable entire site searches by using keywords?

11. Is your website inclined at being promoted by the user among their peers? Does it have enough supporting tools within it?

12. Is your site optimized to be viewed on the trendy new mobile devices so that it could be accessed on the move by this generation's tech savvy user?

13. Has your site's design element been kept simple enough to facilitate loading of content with less or no delays?

14. Is your site smart enough to automate some of you social media engagements but reducing the required levels of intervention?

15. Does your site contain comprehensive measurement and analytics tools to facilitate study of online behaviors of your users?

16. Does your site incorporate any social media monitoring tools to track the level of consumer engagement on a regular basis?

17. Does your website use enough description permalinks in order to increase the scope of your website?

18. Are you able to categorize pages or post to facilitate greater accessing convenience to your end user?

19. Does your website enable the users to easily add metadata to pages without the need to use any technical knowledge?

20. Does your site have any search engine plug-ins and Google site maps built into it?

21. Does your site adhere to rules of search engine optimization techniques so as to attract more traffic onto it?

If you have answered with an affirmative to most of the questions above, your site is ready to take on the social media world challenge. In case there have been questions that you answered with a no in the above questions, I might want to first work on them before taking your journey forward.

SETTING KEY PERFORMANCE INDICATORS

It is never possible to lay enough emphasis on the need to have constant checks in place to monitor progress. In a business environment, it is of utmost importance that all major decisions are taken only after being backed by relevant data. Every business today definitely understands this scenario very well and is in a constant look out for data to facilitate analysis of their performance. Extensive efforts are undertaken to keep an eye on the performance of the business. When such efforts are undertaken to procure data, the business looks at all possible sources. And with huge chunks of data at our disposal on the click of a button, information overload is sure to strike. In light of such an event, it becomes very essential that you determine what will be the performance indicators relevant to your business.

Performance indicators by definition are quantifiable measurements, agreed to beforehand, that reflect the critical success factors of any organization. Just as every business is unique; its performance indicators are also as unique to them. Defining what could be the performance indicators relevant to your business could be tricky but can go a long way if you get it right. So striking the perfect balance becomes very important.

There are many people who believe that performance measurement and performance indicators are just limited to increase in sales or profits but the modern day thinkers differ in their opinions and understanding. They believe that success of any marketing effort by the business cannot be measured by sales figures alone. They believe that progress that can be linked to any effort has to be well rounded. It can be measured by a combination of various factors like increased brand recall, increase in the number of satisfied customers, greater brand loyalty in the customers, etc. Thus came upon the realization in the marketing world that every business has a different kind of indicator in order to measure its performance. Therefore, in order to avoid falling into the common pitfalls of performance measurement it was suggested that performance indicators be segregated based on their importance and relevance to your business. The use of a layered metric structure is an answer to how information overload can be avoided. Layered metrics is nothing but arranging the metrics into tiers based on their importance to your business. A Simple layered structure, metric structure may look like this:

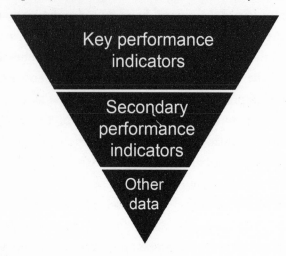

Key performance indicators should be the most critical indicators that focus on the direct relationship of your activity with the outcome. They should cover the major indicators to reflect the performance of your business.

Secondary performance indicators will be the indicators to measure the incidental results to your activity that will pertain to your business. These will be the factors that could be an indicator to your performance without being directly proportionate to it.

Third tier will consist of the other data that you think matters to your business.

After making a clear distinction based on importance and relevance of the factors to the business, it is time to know the factors that needs to be kept in mind while deciding what your key performance indicators should be. You will need to consider the following before you make that list of key performance indicators for your business.

1. Key performance indicators should be aligned well to the desired outcome of your marketing efforts. This is mainly to ensure that your data is relevant to your need. If you get this wrong, you may

end up with a huge chunk of irrelevant data that will do no good to your business.

2. It is important that you look at the entire picture and understand how the key performance indicators you set will drive your organizational progress.

3. They should be set for both micro as well as macro levels in an organization. This is to ensure your expectations from each cluster in your organization like employees, technology etc. is defined.

4. Key performance indicators need to be outcome based and quantifiable.

5. They should be as easy to measure and understand.

6. Key performance indicators should only be a measure of relevant metrics rather than being a sum of all the easily available data.

After considering the above points, list down key performance indicators and the secondary performance indicators relevant for your business. This should act like your check points at every stage in your business to prevent any deviations from your plan.

Now that you have determined your performance indicators, we should shift your focus at developing effective type of content for the various social media platforms.

THINK BEFORE YOU WRITE

Everything said and done, the most bothersome part is to get your interest group to be interested in your content and on the bigger picture, your brand. No matter what strategies are laid out it ultimately boils down into those few moments of attention you gain by your interest group. If you are able to capture this attention of your interest group and give them reasons why they should turn their interest into a buying decision, you have fulfilled your purpose. Honestly, I believe that there could never be any book or guide that could ever guarantee that attention from your interest groups even if they claim so. All that anybody could help you with is a few ideas and guidelines that shall help you when you start out feeling a little more that lost in the wide world of social media. How much these ideas will help is totally up to your imagination. The more you improvise on them to suit your business needs, the better. Taking this discussion further, let us primarily make sense of the buying decision in a general form.

It doesn't matter what marketing book you turn to, any marketing guru will cleave the buying cycle into four stages. Whatever be the terminology used, the idea remains the same. Here, I prefer naming them "The 4 A steps of buying" for our understanding.

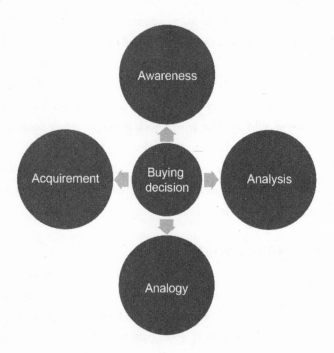

Awareness

The minute your potential customer hears about your brand, he turns into an informed audience. He is aware of your brand and most likely has an idea about what your brand is about. This is the first step- a step towards disseminating information about your brand.

What could you do at this stage?

At the first stage, it becomes important that you keep your potential customer informed about your brand through as many channels as possible. When the customer hears of you through more number of channels, it shall develop a curiosity towards knowing more about your brand. A word of caution here, there is very thin line between informing and irritating the customer. If you come across as a brand trying too hard to sell itself, you may just end up ruining your chances. With the right balance, you could just stir up enough interest towards your brand to achieve greater brand presence.

How you could you do it

On a regular media advertising campaign creating awareness would mean spending more money on ads in television, radio and print. But on this admirable platform of social media, greater efforts take away the prize. It is more about how innovatively you reach your audience. Blowing your own trumpet is not the wise road to take. You need to be smart in a world of smart buyers. So how do you widen your terrain without speaking about your brand? Make the others do the talking for you, get more and more bloggers to review your brand and speak for you. It is human tendency to believe what the third person has to say rather the brand boasting its way in the market. There are bloggers who have a great clout in the social media space. By encouraging them to speak about you, are also taking benefit of the influence they possess in the world of social media. That is a smart way to grab more attention. Apart from this regular social media updates need to be a part of your brand's customer engagement strategy. Keeping the interest groups engaged is a sure way to earn some brownie points.

Analysis

Now assuming that awareness has been created about your brand, what is your customer's next move likely to be? After the curiosity is aroused, a customer may look at knowing more about the brand. He will turn to various sources for such information like friends, word of mouth, industry report, webinars, eBooks, etc. Whatever be the source, he is on the lookout for more enlightenment about your brand.

What could you do at this stage?

When your potential customer is searching for information about you, what else could you provide but more information? Make this stage easier for your potential customer by making the search for information pleasant and easy. Your brand's communication should be convincing but not pushy. Be aware that your customer is smart and will not bear any misrepresentation. Treat him like a smart, well informed individual while you build your content. If you know where your interest group would most likely look for information, setup your guards there. Provide many links to your content and your brand at those places where your interest groups are most likely to flock.

How could you do it?

Develop different forms to your information so that the reach is wide spread, whether your interest group turns to eBooks or webinars you should be able to cater to all. The curiosity aroused in the awareness stage is short lived. It is therefore important to get to the customers information need before the interest dies down. Use content that is easily searchable. Focus on providing the right information at the right time.

Analogizing

Basic human instinct is always about trying to evaluate one thing in terms of another. So be ready to be compared with any near competitors that your brand may have. Analogizing is one way for the customer to assure himself that he's choosing the best available in the market. A customer will compare all the factors important to him among the various brands available before deciding on one.

What could you do at this stage?

While comparing between brands, customers will most likely look for case studies or customer testimonials. They would like to hear from other users or experts about your brand. They believe such sources are more reliable. What could you do here is encourage conversations and comparisons about your brand in social media space instead of shying away from it.

How could you do it?

Just as in the awareness stage we decided on getting more and more people to do the talking for you, follow the same. Encourage reviews of your brand, facilitate discussions and keep your customers engaged. Get your existing customers to write testimonials for you and make them visible to your prospective customers. Invite bloggers who do video demos of any product or service to do it for you. They will also highlight the differences of the brand from the others in the same league. Talk your way!

Acquirement

It is those few moments of purchase when your efforts are tested for their mettle. When a purchase decision is made, it is backed by many conscious and sub-conscious thoughts. With the complexities that the human thinking pattern has to offer, for anybody to decipher each one of those thoughts is a distant dream. But an idea about factors that influence purchase decision does reveal that a positive brand perception is very relevant. At the moment when the customer decides to make that purchase he looks for detailed product information or analyst reports to support his purchase decision.

What could you do at this stage?

You could provide the customer all the technical info that he could possibly ask for. Integrate your content with various analysis reports to increase your trustworthiness. Be there to answer all the doubts that could haunt your customer.

How could you do it?

From specifications to service, leave no unanswered question in your customer's mind. Clarify everything for them to facilitate their decision making process. Clarity of thought needs to be exhibited in your content so that it appeals to a customer and projects your brand as an expert in your domain. Build positive brand image and abide by it.

After understanding what each stage in the buying cycle signifies, let me give you 10 hints on how to write effective content for your social network.

1.   Keep abreast with the industry bulletin.

It is helpful to understand that you are a part of a greater community. Stay informed about the innovative trends of your industry. This will translate into you posting relevant and timely information.

How could you do it?

1. Keep a track on bloggers who cover your industry or who reach out to your interest audience.
2. Keep a tab on those publications exclusive to industry along with your competitors and vendors.
3. Know the keywords that people type-in to search for information in your industry.

With such updates your brand can keep up with all the new developments.

2.   Listen in on those social conversations

Eavesdropping may be considered bad manners but in social media world it promises to do your brand a lot of good. If you begin monitoring the social conversations, it will give you a fair idea of what is general opinion about your brand. You could further on build your strategy based on such real time feedback that you receive. This shall strengthen your brand manifold.

3. Hire a team to create content for your brand

A strong brand message spelled out in different voices will increase the reliability factor for your brand. So hire people to talk for you. Ask them to occasionally blog about relevant areas to your brand. Post short interviews of them to add to your brand's credibility. Get them to give short presentations or webinars. You could explore options outside of your organization as well. You could get freelance writers and editors to take care of creating great content for your brand. The more people speak about you, the better.

4. Create a content backlog and style bank.

When trying to engage your audience on a daily basis, it gets difficult to think of new ideas each day. In order to overcome this difficulty, create a content backlog where you could keep list of topics that you would like to cover. That way you will not have to spend too much time each day pondering about what to write.

Style banks are another great way to ensure great content. You could include things like photos and captions, videos, how to guides, interviews, etc in your style bank. This will give your occasional blog contributors a great place to start without getting lost.

5. Repackage content

Be creative in turning around your existing content into new by reusing it, modifying it and republishing it in another format. Convert your content into different formats. Few ideas has to how you could do this-

1. Turn the plain content into multimedia e-books using new videos
2. Upload speech videos onto YouTube and create discussions around it.
3. Turn your videos into blog posts and eBooks etc.

6.   Use multimedia wherever possible.

Multimedia creates interest on the content like no other media does. Take advantage of this by posting those video blog posts everywhere you think it will work its magic.

7.   Publish yearly posts and "best of" features

When a year worth content is put into concise manner and published, it attracts greater attention. The "best of" features when put together help to capture your brands best moments and put your best foot forward.

8.   Bank on that research data

In the dynamic world ruled by customers, thoroughly researched data shall take your brand a long way forward. When you have your facts right, planning and acting accordingly becomes easy. So make sure you research your data well.

9.   Implement combined relevance

According to social media researcher Dan Zarrella every business customer and prospect has a lot of different interests. When a brand is able to capture those varied interests chances are high to catch their eye. This is a concept of combined relevance. Implement it to benefit from it.

10.   Have an eternal list

When you think there is nothing new are exciting to talk about, it helps to identify some tried and tested topics that never fail to create a buzz. Keep this list handy to give your social web presence the fix it needs from time to time.

Hoping those help, let's try to define the formula for social media success in the next part.

CRSO

DEFINING THE FORMULA FOR SUCCESS

After getting a hang of the buying behavior from the customer point of view, let me now try to elucidate the formula for success in the marketing space of the vast world of social media. As clarified earlier, this is subjective to the uniqueness of your business needs. In marketing terminology when I say "formula of success" I also mean "terms and conditions apply". I have tried to lay down the step by step procedure on how you could go about attaining that success in your social marketing endeavors.

For a quick insight into what the chapter beholds, I have listed down the points that we will bring into light during the course of this chapter. The focus will be to discuss how-to's on certain critical aspects.

- Building a social media team
- Setting up a listening centre
- Creating an engagement cell
- Planning and energizing the campaign
- Building online support mechanism
- Developing a platform to embrace ideas from the customers

Now that you know what you could be reading here, let us move on to unravel each one of these steps and discover what lies within.

BUILDING A SOCIAL MEDIA TEAM

There is certain amount of expertise that is required to do anything when it's paramount to your brand. So my advice here will be for you to set up a Social media team that can solely focus on improving your brand presence in the world of social media. A few things need to be paid attention to while you make your decisions on forming the team. Just as setting up any other team, a social media team needs to able to amalgamate expertise in the various domains that would be essential to social media monitoring. The key challenges that the team should be capable of pulling off with ease would be:

1.   Managing communities

As we spoke about earlier, promoting your brand on the social media platform is a lot different from the regular media marketing. What sets this social media marketing apart is the power of focused attention that could be showered on your interest groups. The world of marketing started out relying on word of mouth that was on a person to person basis in the early stages. Then slowly it graduated to being a more generalized effort by taking benefits of mass advertising. But with time I guess the wheel of marketing has spun its way to personalized marketing efforts again. The customer relationship building and the number of communities built around it has been on the rise. With the advent of social media, these endeavors of the marketing world have been simplified. The boon of the social networking sites to any marketer out there would undoubtedly be the power of effectively communicating with their interest groups. Being able to engage your interest groups on many levels is surely something you don't want to forego.

Your team should be able to build and manage communities on social networking platforms like Facebook, Twitter, LinkedIn etc. They should be able to manage interactions on the various discussion forums as well to benefit from them. The more active part your team plays in building and managing communities, the greater the results from a long term perspective. The network building skills of your team shall be put into test at this stage. If they really are able to increase your clout on the social media platform by being active, there could be nothing better for your brand. The focus here has to be to increase your network reach in the social world.

2.   Engaging and delighting the customer

When the key point is to build a relationship, engaging and delighting the customer has to definitely be on the top of your mind. If increasing the number of fans who follow you is one thing, keeping them constantly interested in your brand is another. Engaging actively with your customer should be the priority for your team in order to make sure you don't lose out on the attention gained from your customer.

As pointed out in chapter 6, the attention span of customers is usually very short. To be able to capture that attention and make the most of it by building a strong relationship with the customer is a huge challenge to any marketer. Your team needs to be creative enough to achieve this by incorporating engagements through customer conversations into your marketing strategy. The other activities that will need to be looked into will be constantly monitoring social conversations about your brand, customer service, etc along with managing promoters' dialogue. In the relationship development point of view, managing the "brand sentiment" is a big league player. The team should be able to develop new ways to create a positive brand sentiment that is compelling enough to influence purchase decision of an individual. The aim at each step should be to delight the customer in every possible way. Such endeavors go a long way forward into developing a strong brand presence for your brand.

3.   Enabling other employees

Your team should be able to take initiatives in helping the other employees. As we discussed in previous chapters, that you need to encourage your employees to write more about relevant content to your brand on various platforms to gain more reliability on the social media platform. When such initiatives are encouraged, the employees will also need to be provided with support at all times. The employees might not really have the skill or the knowledge to write extensively for your brand. This is where the social media team needs to jump in and provide the required support. Along with encouragement, the team should also be able to equip your employees to engage in writing for your organization. Few ideas on how the team could possibly go about enabling other employees are:

a. By setting social media guidelines for the organization:

The team needs to be able to create guidelines for the employees to abide by while they work on creating content for your brand. These guidelines will provide help to those employees who are betwixt and between on how and where to start their writing project.

b. Ensuring consistency in templates, design and tone of the conversation across social media platforms

Due to the fact that you will be encouraging your employees to write about yourself, inconsistency in design or tone is most likely to creep in. Not that they can't do it, but I am just pointing at a possibility of them not being able to deliver effective content due to their lack of experience in writing. This could cause the content to appear disorganized and unappealing to your audience. Hence, here is another chance where the social media team could come into picture and rescue your brand and its personality. The team will need to ensure consistency in template, design and tone of the conversation across the entire social media platform. This shall help to garner the brand personality with qualities like dependable and undeviating.

c. Evaluating engagement / analytical tools for your social media efforts

The social media team shall be responsible to evaluate the outcome of the engagement effort undertaken as per the steps a and b for their effectiveness. They will be responsible to identify the different engagement or analytical tools available in order to check the effectiveness of any engagement effort undertaken.

4. Branding

The social media team should be able to undertake branding exercises for your brand. Since branding is a pretty generic term, I shall list some of the defined ideas on what will need to be covered while taking up branding on social media platform.

a. The team should be able to come up with original ideas giving your marketing effort on the social media a head start.

b. The team should be able to build social media friendly case studies and articles for the benefit of your organization.

c. Content development for multimedia platforms is one area that the team members need to invest on all the available expertise and time.

d. Brand communication as everybody recognizes is a very crucial factor affecting brand sentiment and in turn the brand's personality. Thus the experts in the social media team need to be able to manage all brand communication to ensure that the brand develops a positive presence in the social media world.

5. Analytics

The social media team need to possess the skills required to analyze the results of your brand's marketing efforts on the social media platform. They need to be able to figure out how much impact is your effort creating on your brand's presence and its clout on social media. Some tips on how this could be measured are:

a. They could start by developing or generating metrics that are suited for measuring the impact that your marketing efforts have had on your brand performance.

b. They could also be tracking, reporting the reach and the influence your brand has been able to gather due to your efforts. This could be an analysis of the before and after figures to determine the exact impact. It will give a great insight into the areas that you could improve on in order to better your marketing strategy.

c.   The team can also take the calculation of return on investment into consideration while trying to determine the efficiency of any marketing efforts. This shall help you make sense of how much you have benefited from any marketing strategy that you have undertaken with respect to the amount of money you have put into it. The return on investment alone shall determine if the efforts have been as fruitful as you wanted them to be.

SETTING UP A LISTENING POST

The marketing industry experts, who tried to determine what makes a marketing campaign effective, say that the answer is very simple. I do understand that we are all fascinated by the idea of having complex theories and ideologies to guide us with our marketing efforts rather than some simple logical rule telling us what to do. So what is that simple answer to all our marketing worries? Listening, listening and listening. Though I repeat it three times only to add on to the emphasis, it is the only thing that can take you to being a successful brand. It is very important that you develop a habit of keeping ears open and truly listening to your customers and their needs. There are innumerable clues hidden in every aspect of communication that your customer or your interest group involves in. It is for you to discover them and make sure they work to your advantage. Listen to what people have to say about your brand. Find out what sentiments they associate with your brand. This exercise shall give you great insights into how you could build your brand's personality into being a strong one. Also develop sentiment reports so that you could put a black and white perspective to the kind of brand sentiments that your customers hold for your brand. Once you begin listening to your customer's voices you will start to discover vacuum areas in your efforts that need to be fixed to ensure efficiency.

The gaps could range from being anything like needs and demands of consumers to the dissatisfaction that a customer vents out in the social media space. Whatever be the concern it needs to be paid attention to in order to ensure your customers know that they are being listened to.

Now that you know how important it is to listen, I think you should understand the kind of listening that I am referring to. When I say listening I don't mean the activity of the eardrums alone. I set out to refer to the activity of the brain being able to comprehend whatever is being heard by the eardrums. So I encourage you to stop just hearing and start listening more. There are also certain points that I would like to emphasize about with reference to setting up the listening post.

Listening vs monitoring

Let's briefly compare the word listening to the word monitoring. They are very distinct words. The word monitoring has an impersonal feel to it, while imparting a certain amount of dominance. The word monitoring has a negative connotation attached to it and usually gives people a negative idea. Listening, on the other hand, is a human thing giving a sense of 'being cared for'. And that is exactly what shall do your brand some good.

So how exactly should you listen in on those social conversations? It is not like you walk into a room full of people and listen to what they have to say about you. It is a different arena altogether. It is the newly found path to successful marketing. Just as our every need is answered at a click of the mouse, this one is too. There are several free tools available on the web to enable you to listen to the social conversations that you want to. Some of those free tools are listed below:

- Google alerts
- Technocratic blog search
- Twitter search
- Facebook search
- YouTube search
- Tweetbeep

If you are ready to put in some money into getting advanced tools to help you achieve your purpose, the web also has some great options to offer. Some of the popular paid listening tools are:

Meltwater Buzz: If you are looking for something to be able to help you in comprehensive tracking and analysis of user-generated content, look no further. Meltwater Buzz is great for this requirement. (www.buzz.meltwater.com)

Parature: If you would like to have the customer comments routed to appropriate departments with minimal or no human intervention, Parature is what you have been on the lookout for. It is great to let the customer comments directly reach the department instead of being pushed around without it reaching the correct destination. Any comment that does not make it to the concerned department is as good as not having any comments from the customer. In fact it does even more damage as the customer feels he is being ignored and this is not good for your brand. So I think if you are ready to invest on Parature, there shall be no regret.(www.parature.com)

Radian6:   Are of the opinion that your brand will benefit from doing much more that just listening? Would you like to be able to measure and also analyze your social media efforts? Would you like to truly engage with your customers? If you find yourself answer in affirmatives for the above then I can safely assume that you are on a lookout of a great tool to reach these targets. Radian6 is one such tool that provides the ability to do it all. It offers an excellent tool for listening, measuring and engaging with your customers across the entire social web.(www.radian6.com)

Sysomos: If you are the kind of person who needs to act upon any thought instantly and do not like to be kept waiting or doesn't like any kind of delays, Sysomos is the tool for you. It is a good tool that provides instant and unlimited access to all social media conversations that you could ever ask for. (www.sysomos.com)

Crimson Hexagon: Would you like to gather social media information that directly or indirectly affects your brand or its presence? Crimson Hexagon is that tool that provides you this power. It is an excellent tool to gather that social media intelligence that you value so much.(www.crimsonhexagon.com)

Now that you know what are the options available at your disposal

a.   Write down a list of five phrases people might use that would identify themselves as potential customers of yours. Conduct Twitter and Facebook searches for each of these phrases.

b.   Conduct Twitter, YouTube and Facebook searches for your brand, competitors, products and services. Take note of what people are saying about you.

c.   Develop a plan and system to formally or informally listen on a daily basis throughout the social web, and determine ways your organization can benefit from the insight gained by listening.

Now that we are clear on the kind of listening that I am referring to and how you could use the available web listening tools for your benefit, let us answer some critical questions on listening to clear up any more doubts that you might have.

WHY SHOULD YOU LISTEN?

- Listening helps in building your marketing strategy as a two way communication process. It facilitates you to understand
- What your customers or interest groups think about you?
- What is the brand sentiment your interest group associates with your brand?
- What does you present social media presence say about your brand?
- What are the messages that you are sending out to your interest group both consciously and subconsciously?

Answering these questions will help you do the ground work for your social media strategy that you wish to undertake.

What you should pay attention to?

When you take that plunge into the social media world you will most probably find yourself hovering around in a vast pool of information from so many sources. In order to prevent finding yourself in such a situation, try dividing your listening into various categories for more clarity. The categories could be based on factors like what you are listening to. The categories should covered areas like:

1. Discontentment expressed by your customers
2. Appreciations showered on your brand by your customers
3. Enquires put forward by your customers or interest groups
4. Any leads that you could follow and act upon
5. Conversations that provide an opportunity to promote your brand
6. Any needs that have been put forth by your customer that you could meet
7. Any data on the competitors and their strategic moves
8. Any information that could give you a hint as to what kind of content attracts visitors to your brand's space
9. Identify influential bloggers within the ambit of your services
10. Any words that could serve as an early warning system to you before any issues that consumers are facing with your brand goes mainstream
11. Definitely listen to what your return on investment is on this strategy in order to decide if it is working well as you want it to be.

Where to listen?

As I always emphasize on the need to recognize that every organization is unique and everything about it is unique as well. Does that mean I shall not lend you any tips? Of course I will. My advice to you will be to start using a set of tools from the above mentioned list. That shall help you to cover the entire area of social web and also reveal to you the needs of your business. As time passes you will be able to tell the difference between what works for your brand and what doesn't.

Due to the dominance of Facebook and Twitter in the social media world today people often mistake them to be the only constituents of this wide world. You need to understand that social web platforms are much more that those two websites. In the context of your business it could range from being a niche online community like LinkedIn to being blogs on relevant topics. The variety is huge and it is up to your business to make the most of it by analyzing what your interest group might be using as pointed out in chapter 6.

Who should take care of these activities?

Ideally as we have already discussed, you should have a social media team to look after all these activities. But if you think you would like to make use of your existing resources rather than spending on hiring new ones, you could involve in it yourself or your employees. In this approach you should be able to assign each function to the selected employees while keeping in mind two things. The selected individual should have the interest along with the skill to handle the function assigned to him. Secondly it should not in any way affect his current functional role. There will be some employees in every organization who exhibit a lot of enthusiasm in undertaking the social media project. Encourage them and facilitate their efforts in all possible ways to get the best of them.

How should you listen?

When asked such a question the first picture that we usually tend to see is a person standing behind a door and listening in on the conversation in the room. Since we are particularly talking about social media you can't really do that. So how else can you? In the social world you will need a plan to do it. How do you think you should plan in order to take on in this world? How can you exactly get what you are searching for? I would advise you to categorize your search on a macro level. You could search about

- your brand
- your industry
- your competitors

Your brand

When searching for your brand you will need to focus your searches on the words or phrases that are directly related to your brand. In order to help here, you could come up with a stack of keywords or phrases that talk about

- Your brand
- Your products and services
- Your specialties
- Your marketing strategy
- Synonyms of the above

Your industry

If you come across as a proactive brand who studies the industry well, it will help your brand's personality a lot. Industry listening will help stay in touch with the larger picture that includes the environment that surrounds your business as well as the happening gossip that could help you. Your search could include factors like:

- Words that describe you specialties
- Markets that your brand is able to cover
- Broader industry keywords
- The new market opportunities that your brand is keenly looking out for
- Your thought leaders in the industry
- All the emerging trends in your industry

This search should help you establish your foothold in your industry and also establish your online presence on the social media platform.

Your competitors

Competitor analysis promises to throw open greater opportunities to any brand. To benefit from it, your search should aim at revealing the following factors that could help you in your business.

a. Any basic information about your competitors

b. What are the factors that differentiates your competitor from your brand

c. What attracts the customers to your competitor brands

d. What are your competitors doing differently in term of marketing strategies and efforts

e. What could you learn from your competitor brands in order to make your brand better with each passing day?

I have been warning you and will warn you again here- Don't ever confuse listening with just hearing. Listening is more of an activity which is all about engaging your customer. So what exactly is engagement in this context?

By definition the word engagement is to occupy the attention or efforts of a person or people. Engaging your customer can never be a onetime thing. It is a series of continuous efforts put in order to capture your audience and compel them to listen to what your brand communication has to say.

WHY IS ENGAGEMENT IMPORTANT FOR YOUR BRAND?

There are two things that conversations about you can do to your brand. One thing being the optimistic way of having people talking good about your brand and praising your service which shall in turn add that positive sentiment to your brands personality on the whole. This if achieved shall prove to be a very effective marketing tools for any brand. It ensures that doors to different avenues open up to your brand due to the strong brand sentiment held among the interest groups of any brand.

If the odds are against a brand, you may find people posting complaints about the brand and its services on the social media. Such an outburst tends to spread like wildfire and needs to be kept under watch and controlled in time. In the first positive scenario, the brand can sit back and muse at the fruits of its marketing efforts however the second scenario calls for damage control. Whenever there seems to be a possibility of the second scenario striking it becomes very important that a brand takes adequate steps to minimize the damage to brand image. When such negative cases are noticed during the regular social media monitoring session either by a brands social media team or by its employees, immediate action needs to be taken. The brand will have to make efforts to exhibit to the dissatisfied customer that their woes and opinions are being listened to. If the customer is not pacified at this stage by showering the necessary attention and concern to their experiences, there is a possibility of the situation getting out of hand. Thus a brand will need to ritualistically try and listen to any such situations on the social media platforms at all times. At a preventive measure to avoid such cases the brand could also act proactively. The brand can start by collecting regular and timely feedback about them from the customer either actively or passively. This is exactly why engagement is important for your brand.

As a brand you might wonder what would be the appropriate things to be said in such situations. My advice here would be that customer will always appreciate honest and simple replies. Your replies reflect your sincerity and your assurance to see that the incident shall never repeat itself. Such a response will calm the enraged customer. You could say things like:

- We apologize for the inconvenience caused to you
- We are thankful that you brought this issue to our notice
- We are grateful for your support
- Please feel free to let us know how we can help you further
- We would love to hear from you

Now breaking this down to five ways on how to have a great social media monitoring plan to enhance customer engagement

1. Decide on the areas you wish to focus your attention.
2. Make sure to articulate your goals and measurements
3. Consider the resources that you have in hand
4. Map the information flow for your convenience
5. Illustrate the steps at each stage along with the results you are expecting out of them.

Where to engage?

The answer to this question shall always remain - Go where your interest group goes to. Where else will they find you? I am sure you definitely will agree with me on this, don't you?

So how exactly do you build a strong engagement strategy?

From the point of view of your brand, firstly establish guidelines that give those engaging with your customers the freedom to improvise while representing your brand without actually overstepping any lines.

When getting involved in conversations about your industry and the verticals that you serve, you should try and establish your brand as a thought leader in your industry. While doing so you should also try to come across as a brand that really cares for the community as well as it customers.

Competitive engagement is not about slinging mud on your competitor. It is more about bringing out the points of differentiation that your brand possesses in comparison to your competitor brands.

Practice conversational listening to excel in your engagement efforts. When you inculcate the practice of conversational listening in your daily engagement efforts, you are also building a strong relationship with your customer. This relationship is sure to take you a long way. Conversational listening also sends out a positive message to your audience saying you value their thoughts and are listening to what they have to say. It personalizes your brand to the customer like no other marketing effort does It is your way of letting the consumer know that you 'care' and 'listen' to them. You can always delight your customers by reaching out to them when they need your help. We could thus be moving towards, pro-active customer service. That is, reaching the customer even before he calls the helpline!

Now that the listening post is up, let us move on to the next step.

Setting up an engagement cell along with choosing your social media wisely

It is essential that you understand how important it is to be able to engage with your customers on the social media platform. So let us revisit why you will need a separate social engagement cell.

It is a hard fact that customers don't label themselves. It is really none of their concern of how your organization chooses to handle customer relationship. All that they need is that they should not be sent running from pillar to post when they are in need of something. This is all that matters to them. So how an organization handles this is not what they are bothered about. They just want to be listened to in that moment of need. In their eyes your entire organization is one and they don't pay heed to the differentiation in terms of departments that your organization might have. What that means in terms of engagement is that you're going to have a hard time trying to engage with one sector of your community, but not another. But once you've opened the door to communicating and engaging with your community, they're going to want to talk to you, no matter where in your customer brackets they fall under.

Blogging is another popular method that organizations use in order to make their mark on the social media platform. Even in this way you are sure to have people leaving comments and at the same time wanting to be responded back to. They are surely not typing out those words into the outer space without expecting any reply; they are talking to you and want to be talked back to. So it doesn't matter what social media strategy you put in place, people will always want you to respond back. After so much said about how response is so very important and that people expect it from you, you might be thinking this is going to be hard. But let me educate you by saying it is going to be a good thing for your brand. Here's how you can turn this around and work your way to a good engagement strategy.

This is exactly why I shall recommend you to have a social engagement cell. We surely understand that asking your regular employees to handle your entire engagement strategies can be exhausting on them too. And the fact also remains that it is highly unlikely that you will be able to create those marketing miracles without put in your 100 % effort into it.

If you spend the time and effort to listen and monitor, you'll be able to identify trends in the conversation and understand what your customers might be expecting from you. The information that you gather through listening becomes the foundation for your engagement strategy.

Also you will need to realize that once you engage with your community, going back is hard. When you throw in your opening lines it is like an open invitation for people to come and talk about or to your brand. Your engagement cell will have to put in a lot of effort to be there all the time for people out there. But don't let that deter you. Use your listening practices strategically. Take the time to inform yourself and your engagement cell about all the what-ifs of engagement for your company and how your interest group is likely to react when you start conversing with them.

That way, instead of getting a shock by the magnitude of the number of people who want to talk to you, your engagement cell be able to confidently and consistently connect with your customers, wherever they are, and evolve your engagement strategy along the way.

Energizing to boost sales

Due to the fact that you are willing to take your social media marketing so seriously, I see how motivated you are to boost your sales. It is great to have that kind of motivation driving you at each step. Social media offers a wider platform than ever to be able to generate leads and thus in turn boosting your sales. But of course nothing in this world comes for free. If you have just gotten the impression that you have to pay to be on social media platform, I think I shall clarify that statement. I mean that social media platform needs you to put in a lot of effort before you reap benefits in the long run. I guess the saying "you reap what you sow" in any context could never have been so apt.

Customer service on social media

As already discussed social media offers you to address your customers concerns and grievances in the shortest possible time in order to help in achieving a high standard in customer servicing for your brand. Such a great strategy can help your brand get the best of brand loyalty into its kitty from the customers. Thus I can never emphasize more on achieving high levels of service to your customers through social media platforms. Great way to tag along the positive adjective in your brand personality I should say!

INNOVATING THROUGH EMBRACING IDEAS FROM CONSUMERS

When you get the tips right from the horse's mouth could you ever ask for more? Being able to listen to the needs of your customer in his own words can any day beat all those endless hours of need recognition sessions every organization undertakes in order to be able to develop new products. When you know how you could innovate through embracing ideas from your consumer, you have surely mastered the skill of listening to the master (in your case it shall be your customer).

When social media offers so much stacked up on its platter, the ultimate results solely depend on how best you implement these strategies.

As I endeavor to make your journey onto social media platform simple and easy, here I present you with 25 tips that you should surely pay heed to make your social presence remarkable.

1. Start building inbound links into content in order to be more searchable by the various search engines. You could get more people to link back on your website by creating high-quality content, submitting your website to online directories, writing guest posts for various blogs, etc.

2. Recognize the need to emphasize on keywords to enable social media optimization on your website. List the keywords and try to include them as much as possible in your website's content.

3. Try and incorporate title tags as well as meta tags for your content so that search engines can easily find you. Don't worry if you have no clue about the coding involved behind this, most website editors and content management systems enable you to easily edit meta tags without coding knowledge.

4. Add XML sitemaps to your website so that search engines can swift run through your content more effectively. XML sitemaps are nothing but a defined form to the data that you have on your site along with details on when you last updated your content. This again could be easily done with the help of sitemap generators that are found online.

5. We all surely have experienced trying to click on a web address and being answered with a "Page not found" message. This is an example of lost opportunity caused due to not using a permanent 301 Redirect, a method used to link your old web address to new one. Make certain you do it.

6. First impression is crucial. When a visitor visits your site the first impression that you create will surely be a lasting one. So get your design elements right to create that right impression. In focusing on your design you will also need to make sure that you are not neglecting on the quality of the content as well.

7. As we have already discussed on this, you will need to focus on maintaining consistency in your content throughout.

8. To make your website visually appealing use the right kind of

pictures. They surely make a lot of difference.

9. Keep the navigation system on the site simple and easy in order to facilitate hassle free browsing within your site.

10. Don't go overboard with the use of flash or animation on your site as they increase the loading time for the pages and may cause the visitor to leave sooner. Limit it to wherever necessary only.

11. Make your website compatible to all kinds of viewing in order to attract more visitors.

12. Keep your content crisp and easy to grasp.

13. Include a lot of educative content that can add value to your websites as well as its visitors.

14. Always choose quality over quantity when it comes to your content.

15. Avoid using too many jargons in your content.

16. Clarity is what captures the audience. It could be the clarity in your site design or the clarity of thought that you exhibit within your content. So be clear on what you want to convey.

17. Might sound like extra homework to you, but creating a blog will benefit your brand a lot.

18. Make your content shareable and social as much as possible.

19. Incorporate multiple forms of data in your content to create a content-rich experience.

20. Get customers to write testimonials for you. A customer is more likely to believe a fellow customer.

21. Highlight the next steps that you want your customer to take on your website. This in technical language is called Call to Action (CTA). This shall increase the possibility that they will ideally follow that route that you want them to.

22. Place your CTA's is appropriate place on your website.

23. In the next level of a user's browsing about on your site try to convert them to leads by collecting some details about them in the landing page which follows the CTA's.

24. The keys to the landing page will be forms. Get your visitors to fill

in forms with fewer fields so that it doesn't feel like too much work. It is feels like too much work they are most likely to back out.

25. Newsletters are another great way of tapping the inboxes of your interest groups more often. So don't forget to get your visitors to sign up for newsletters from your website.

Now that is about how you could create a website that drives traffic, generates leads and most importantly boosts the sales figures. Next up will be the answer to the question "How to choose platform and measure success".

CRWSO

CHOOSING PLATFORMS
AND MEASURING SUCCESS

No matter how much information you gather about how to make it big on the social media platform, the fact shall remain that none of it could make that important decision for you or your brand. The important decisions are to be taken within the ambit of dilemmas of choosing what could work for your brand. You are bound to agree with me when I say that what work brilliantly for somebody else might not really be your way to success. As I always keep emphasizing on the fact that your marketing strategy on social media will have to be just as unique to you as your brand itself is. So there is no hard and fast rule book that could work for you. It has to be you who shall work on figuring out your best move and act accordingly.

The first and foremost thing that you would need to decide will be the right platform for your brand. Due to the fact that your interest groups are varied, you will have to make your decision based on where web choices. This is to avoid situations like the ones below:

1. Your interest group have people in the age bracket of 50 to 60 years and you have made your plans for social media using YouTube videos or Twitter

2. Your interest group have school going kids and you decide to advertise on new born supply websites.

To avoid such social media blunders you will need to make sure, that you make your platform choices after a lot of research and deliberation. List all the factors that could affect your choice of platform and base your decision on these factors..

The decision once made does not always have to hold good due to change in needs and times. It therefore becomes very important for any brand to constantly keep an eye on the performance of their devised social media plan to check if it is doing good or will require any improvisation. To serve this purpose of constant checking, social media marketing analytics becomes very essential.

Social media marketing analytics by definition is the discipline that helps measure, assess as well as explain the performance of social media initiatives in the context of specific objectives that the brand has set for itself to achieve. The metrics that each brand uses is different based on its needs. They could be varied based on factors like:

1. The amount of conversation buzz that the brand is able to create on the social media platform.

2. The proposed value that each conversation that the brand undertakes has.

3. The volume of conversations that the brand is able to have across various social media entities like Blogposts, forums, discussions, tweets, Facebook status updates and many more.

4. The coverage that the brand exhibits within its social media reach across all demographics.

5. The level of influence that the brand possesses over its interest groups.

6. The message reach that the brand has earned for itself

7. The sentiment that the brand has been able to develop among its consumers. This could be measured by the positive or negative attitudes expressed by the consumers over various platforms.

8. The share of voice of a particular brand heard in an industry discussion scenario.

9. The common topics that the brands talk about while trying to engage its consumers.

10. The viral factor that the brand might posses translates into speedy spread of messages conveyed by the brand to its customers.

Those are some of the general metrics that could be the basis to any social media marketing analytics exercise. And if you are looking at some metrics that are specific to the platform that you are using on the social media space, here goes:

1. **Facebook** – You could measure your performance on Facebook by basing your analysis on the number of fans, number of likes, number of shares or the number of members in the communities that you create.

2. **My Space** – On this platform you could use measures like number of friends along with the number of comments to any of your posts or content.

3. **LinkedIn** – In this kind of platform your measuring factor shall be the number of recommendations along with the number of connections that you were able to generate among your interest group.

4. **Twitter** – On Twitter you could use the number of people following your brand, the number of people you follow, favorites etc. as your data for analysis of how successful you are on social media.

5. **YouTube** – On this platform you could use indicators like number of views, number of subscribers, comments, discussions about your content, ratings etc.

Now coming to a more structured social media measurement framework, there are going to be four steps to it, which are:

Planning the exercise

Planning the exercise will include all those steps of putting in writing what you will need to do in order to carry on according to your game plan. In fact it is a stage where you shall actually devise your game plan. While you are at this, you will need to keep in mind that this step shall prove to be the foundation to your plan, it shall be one of the determining factors whether your efforts will be a success or not.

Defining the metrics

Defining the metrics is surely important because you will have to determine the scale that you would use to measure your success beforehand. Some people are of the opinion that it is not so important to actually lay down the metrics. According to them, the success of an effort shall reflect on the sales figure and that is how they prefer to be informed about the return on their investments. However I would slightly beg to differ here. According to me, there are lot of factors that need to act in harmony in order to led those sale figures soar high. So it can be a daunting task to actually pin point which factor is directly proportional the sales numbers. There could be many factors behind the rise or fall of these numbers. So it shall be wise to actually define what is it that you intend to measure your progress against. Whenever you decide to know, where you have reached through your efforts and also how far you are from your goal, the defined metrics help you to scale it. A word of caution here, you will need to put your over optimism to rest before you take this step. It is very important that you define your metrics with loads of realistic goals so that you get the exact picture at all times.

Implementing the plan

Implementing the plan shall be the next step after you are done with your groundwork. You will need to remember that no plan is perfect. Every plan can just take a shot at perfection however there will still be some loopholes that shall creep in without you noticing them. These are not to be taken as faults in the plans. They need to be treated with the dignity of natural occurrences. After that level of acceptance dawns up on you it shall become even more important that you find your ways to deal with them. So, go ahead, take the plunge while keeping your eye for those natural flaws that might have crept in. Learn more to deal with those flaws rather than complaining about them.

Identifying technology tools

Identifying tech tools will be the phase where you will have to choose the best tech tools for you. From addressing your bare minimum needs to your unexpressed needs, technology has a solution to all. It is therefore necessary to identify the various tech tools that you will need to keep you company while you are on your path to your goal. Explore a lot of options and be sure to choose the one that suits you the best. The effort to find the most suitable tools shall never go waste.

MEASUREMENT OF SOCIAL ENGAGEMENTS

Why measure social engagements?

On any path that you take in life you will need those constant checks in place just to keep you informed if you are on the right track. Knowing that you are on the right path at every step will ensure that you don't have to rework all that would be required to get back onto the correct track after you discover that you have lost your way.

The lesser the time taken to identify any deviations from the plan, the better for your business plan. When any aberration is discovered in the working of any factors of your marketing plan, a quick action method will help your brand go a long way. So in order to act quickly to minimize any damage done, you will need to have concrete measurement tools in place. These tools should be able to tell you exactly where you are headed to. That is the level of importance that measurement at every stage carries for your business.

What do we have to look for when we measure social engagements?

After knowing why your brand requires to measure the social engagements that have resulted directly or indirectly due to its marketing efforts. To be able to measure your brands social engagements it become imperative for you to understand what your organization wants to accomplish and what market you want to target. This will help to determine what metrics are actually relevant to your brand. You will need to establish both qualitative and quantitative measurements for your goals because both matter in providing a complete picture of the progress of your social media program.

While you are doing so, it is crucial that you remember not to settle for measuring only outputs and outtakes. The impact or the quantifiable changes in attitude, behavior and opinion will be measured only when your measuring strategy is based upon considering various factors and outcomes. There have also been brands that have been sucked into measuring superficial results such as number of followers or fans; this shall directly result in their social media and engagement strategy's success akin to a mirage in the dessert. It is therefore necessary that you understand that you have to protect yourself from falling into the easy measurement traps. Anything to succeed will require efforts, so will your social media engagement strategy and its measurement. Some ideas on what you should ideally be measuring to measure what factor has been listed for your convenience.

To determine the effects on the revenue and business development of your business, you could set your metrics with factors like

- Customer Retention per cent
- Value of transactions
- Referrals that you are able to generate
- Net New Leads
- Cost Per Lead
- Conversions from Community

To determine the effects on the activity levels and engagement of your brand with your customers, you could set your metrics with factors like

- Number of members or fans
- Number of posts or threads related to your brand
- Comments or ideas that your interest groups express to you

- Inbound links within your content
- Tags, Votes, Bookmarks for your content
- Active Profiles on your brands page
- Referrals that you are able to generate
- The frequency with which your interest group posts on your webspace

To determine the effects on the cost savings that your business is able to achieve, you could set your metrics with factors like

- The time that your business takes to resolve any issues that your customers or interest groups might have
- The percentage of Issues Resolved Online through any effective social monitoring plan
- Account turnover that your business has been able to achieve
- Employee turnover rate that your business faces during its course
- The costs that your business spends on hiring or recruiting new people
- Training costs that your business incur to help the new joinees
- New product ideas that your business has embraced and succeeded from
- Development cycle time that your business takes to develop a new product or plan for a new service

To determine the effect value awareness and influence that your brand is able to gather, you could set your metrics with factors like

- The brand loyalty or affinity that your brand commands among the industry consumers
- Media placements that your brand is subjected to
- The frequency of conversation sharing about your brand
- The sentiment that the various posts about your brand reflect
- The Net Promoter Score of your brand

CREATING A SOCIAL MEDIA PLAN

While looking to create a social media plan, it is very important that you get your basic steps right. So before embarking on that journey you will have to start with the following steps:

Determining your brands objectives

For any brand to succeed it is very important that you know what are the objectives that shall guide you throughout. Do remember to keep it Specific, Measurable, Attainable, Realistic/Relevant, and Timely (SMART)

Do your Research well

Develop a list of social media sites where you can potentially engage with people. The list will most likely start off with Twitter, Facebook, LinkedIn, and a few select blogs and forums. Check out each of the social media sites on your list and do additional research to determine relevancy by searching for your brand name, your competitors, and your target keywords. Listen to what's out there, identify, and understand your target audience.

Make a list of contacts and content

When social media is used correctly, relationships will build naturally. Begin making connections by following the conversation. You can do this by subscribing to blogs in your industry and by making a list of influencers who are relevant to your business. This becomes handy when it's time to provide content on your social networks.

Join the Conversation to Develop Relationships

Now it's time to start making use of all the research you've done. You can start joining the conversation by posting comments on blogs and forums, answering questions on Yahoo! and LinkedIn, joining groups related to your industry and joining Twitter chats. Begin developing relationships by following and befriending influencers and those in your industry.

Strengthen Relationships

Make extensive efforts to build and maintain great relationships online.

Measure Results

You have goals and objectives, right? That means you should be able to measure your success. Remember, what you measure will tie into the goals and objectives of your social media strategy.

Let's take the four commonly used objectives:

- Improve brand presence across social channels — The measurement goal here is an increase in the number of followers on Twitter, number of fans on Facebook, number of comments, number of times your brand is mentioned in blogs and forums and so on.

- Increase positive sentiment about your brand — The goal here is to convert the number of positive mentions while taking note of negative mentions.

- Develop relationships for future partnership opportunities — This goal is to keep track of those with whom you've connected.

- Increase traffic to your website — Keep track of visitors to your website who come from each of your social media sites

Analyze, Adapt, and Improve

Your social media strategy doesn't end with measurement; it goes beyond that. You need to analyze your social media campaigns, adapt any new findings into your current processes, and improve your efforts.

After knowing what it shall take to create a successful social media strategy, let us now get our hands dirty and actually get down to doing it. The most important aspects of the social media plan for any business shall include the following steps:

1. Setting objectives for your social media campaign
2. Setting up an active listening mechanism for your brand
3. Putting in place an engagement mechanism that is most suited for your brand
4. Making that decision of choosing the right platforms for your brand
5. Getting around to measuring your success using various metrics that you set for yourself

If you have looked closely enough, you would have noticed that the first three points have already been spoken about in the previous chapters. So I think I shall not really repeat myself there. Assuming that is ok, I shall move further on to the main focus of this chapter as well as the next point in line after the first three.

CHOOSING THE RIGHT PLATFORMS FOR YOUR BRAND

Now that the engagement mechanism and its goals have been fixed, you will need to take time out to evaluate what all the world of social media has to offer and make that decision of choosing the right platforms to use for your brand. However, choosing the platform isn't as easy as it may sound. It is very important that you ensure that you reach the right audience thereby increasing the chance of your campaign going viral. In order to help with that, let us first quickly have a look at what are the important factors that can help you in choosing the right platforms for your brand.

The checklist that shall help you get through this Herculean task of choosing the right platform will be as follows

1. The corporate goals that you have set for your business.
2. The objectives that you have set for your business.
3. The measures that you have determined to ensure you are on the right path to achieve your goals.
4. The channels that you plan to use while you focus on getting your message through to your interest group.

The various corporate goals that any business will stand for are innovation, customer loyalty, employee loyalty, customer acquisition and most importantly revenue generation. Once this is set hard in concrete everything else shall fall in place.

1. Any business needs to set its objectives in such a way that it is inclusive of factors that spur innovation, promote advocacy, facilitate support and generate interactions, foster dialogue about your brand and also gains exposure for your brand.

2. There are also measures that will help you stay in connect with the industry. You could do that by studying those trends in the various factors like brand sentiments that your customers connect to and also the various ideas that impact your business for good.

3. You will also be able to find those influencers online who are actively spreading their word in your industry. These influencers are the ones that people turn to when they need advice on something or need to make a choice between two brands. Keeping an eye on what such individuals have to say about you will help your brand a lot. These individuals have a significant impact on developing brand loyalty for your brand. They can be found on the various platforms in the social media world. You will need to do all that you can to get them to talk about your brand so that your brand benefits from them.

4. Also focus your attention on the resolution rate that your brand has exhibited in the past and how you could possibly better it. You will have to make sure that you are constantly improving the resolution time that your business takes to resolve any issues raised by your customers. This constant endeavor will help your brand a lot.

5. From the point of view of your customers you could get to know what they think by asking them to score you. When you ask your customer to rate your product or service based on the satisfaction that you have delivered, it gives you the accurate picture of your brand from the view point of a customer. The satisfaction score shall also tell you the areas that your brand needs to focus on. Depending on scores you can focus your attention on improving on the areas that your brand lacks in. What better way to improving your brand as well as its image?

6. When the importance that you shower your customer with increases, the conversion rate from an individual being just interested in you to actually making that purchase increases manifold. When the conversion rate is high it translates into being a great return on investment to all your marketing efforts.

7. You will also need to keep an eye on the interaction rate that you maintain with your existing customers as well as your prospective customers. This will help you reach out to your customers whenever you need to or whenever they need you. As simple as it may sound, it surely is an important call for any business in this highly competitive world.

8. Another important factor that promises the sky for any business is the activity of measuring the volume of conversations that it initiates with its customers. The higher the volume of conversations, the greater the benefit to any brand. Constantly keeping in touch with customers enable the business to identify the customer's needs as and when they express it on the social media space.

9. A brand's engagement is an indicator to its relationship with its audience. A healthy relationship is exhibited by a strong engagement strategy. When the brand actually connects with the customer and also enables the customer to connect to them, they are sure to head towards being a very strong brand in very short span of time.

10. The reach that the brand has is directly related to the wide spread of marketing communication channels that the brand resorts to in order to get its brand message across to its customers. It can also be seen as the dominance that a brand exhibits in the marketing space. This measure also includes the factor of how diverse the brands customers are and how popular the brand is in comparison to its peers from the industry.

11. The velocity with which the brand message reaches the interest group of the brand is very crucial. The faster the communication channel, the more effective the communication will be.

12. The share of voice that your business possesses among your peers in the industry shall help determine how influential your brand is in the market space. If your brand exhibits a high share of voice it means that your brand possess thought leadership in the industry. This can also mean that you could be the market leaders in the

industry. Being a market leader in their respective industry needs to be on every brands hit list.

So what are the various tactics that every brand adopts in order to achieve the corporate objectives that they set for themselves.

Forums: Brands today have turned into smart brands by turning to consumer forums instead of tedious sessions in order to come up with new product innovations with the view to satisfy the customer. When the brands are able to get the needed information right from the horse's mouth, will there be any other better way to do the same? Smart brands say no. They engage in all forms of communication including forums and discussions as a solution to the communication hurdles that they face.

Communities: Another trend that is catching on in the fast world today is the trend of creating communities. When I say communities I mean the online communities that are actively involved in activities ranging from discussions to opinion polls. These communities are a great way to find that niche interest group who might be the right audience to your brand. This is exactly what any brand would look for when on the lookout for the perfect place to speak about themselves to reach the right set of people. It is a more targeted approach that offers better chances in comparison to any general marketing efforts.

Social media platforms: The reach that social media platform offers is just so vast that it wasn't possible to even imagine its impact until a few years ago. The kind of reach that businesses are taking benefit of it is a mix between information penetrations with a dash of word of mouth marketing effect.

An own brand website: When a prospective customer hears about a brand, he looks around to find more about it. In the Google ruled world today, it is inevitable that they will come to look your brand up on the search engine site. When the interest reaches this level it is up to the brand to put its best foot forward and capture the customer's interest. What better way to do this than speak for yourself instead of having only third party conversations about the brand. When a brand has a presentable website it speaks oodles about the brand itself. The kind of message that the website communicates can be both verbal or feel based. Thus the brands tend to take this route to reach out to their consumers.

Based on the tactics (or social media channels) adopted for every corporate objective you can choose the platform you'd like to use.

You will first need to classify all the popular platforms in the geographical area into 4 categories: Expressing, Networking, Sharing and Gaming. Based on the target audience and the priority of the basket, you could select those that you will use for the campaign.

Now that you have chosen the right platforms, it is important to define the key performance index (KPI's), which may be challenging but is critical. KPI's must provide context, set expectations and mandate actions. Let us begin with setting foundational measures for success – measures that will help us gain high-level insights too. As already discussed very often we base the success of social media campaigns on:

- Visits to our website
- Page views
- Number of Likes
- Number of shares

Unfortunately, these fail to completely define the success achieved. In many cases, it acts as a deterrent for your brand to make the best of social media.

So, here are the fundamental things you will need to measure your success with:

Interactions: The first and foremost factors that you can turn to are interactions on the social media world. Theses interactions can be derived from analyzing conversations and activity of your brand on the social media platform.

Engagement: The next factor that could help you measure your success will be the social audience engagement that your brand has been able to do. Engagement can be derived from the combination of number of visits, time spent, comments and shares.

Influence: A very important factor to measure your success on social media world shall be calculating the influence your brand exercises on your interest group. This measure can be discovered by measuring the volume of relevant content, comments on it, its 'shares' and its reach.

Advocates: Another factor that you could consider would be the advocates that your brand possesses. Advocates are individuals who 'influence' your brand presence on Social Media in a positive way. They not only read your content but leave positive comments and also share it with their friends. It is a factor that can be defined by combining Influence and positive sentiments.

Impact: The last but not the least factor that you could use will be the measure of the impact that your brand creates on the social media world. This can be judged by knowing the outcome, interactions and engagement of the

MEASURING SUCCESS

Before we begin engaging users on social media and draw analytics or metrics; it's important to decide, as early as possible, how success will be measured. Generally, there can be only two types of outcomes from social media that can be used to define (or measure success)

Financial outcomes:

The financial outcomes of an effort can be translated into various changes that includes, cost reduction and increased revenue. A few examples on how this can manifest into are:

i.   Increase in sales during a social media campaign

ii. Sales that comes from new customers acquired though social media campaigns

iii. Reduction in cost by shifting a portion of customer service tickets to social media channels like Twitter

Non-financial outcomes:

The outcomes of your social media campaign can also be non-financial in nature. In the sense of not involving any money terms they can range from any of the below examples:

i.   An incre   in unique website visitors

ii.   A change in positive mentions

iii. A change in negative mentions

iv.   Net new Facebook fans

v.   Net new Twitter followers

vi.   Net new requests for information

vii. An increase in RSS subscriptions

viii. An increase in visits to the retail outlets

ix.   Increased time spent on the website

x.   A change in volume of impressions

xi.   A reasonable increase in YouTube video downloads

xii. The number of times an article was liked and shared

xiii. The number of comments on a blog post

So how exactly does the sequence of events take place to fit in financial and non financial gains into the picture?

For a clearer understanding let us first know the components of this flow. The components are as below:

- Investment
- Action
- Reaction
- Non-financial impact
- Financial impact

Investment: The initial amount of money invested in social media campaigns will be termed as the investments put in by the business. For example: Buying ads on Facebook page. Let's say: Rs.10, 000

Action: This is the stage where in the brand is trying to create its presence on social media. An example of this shall be: Starting a Facebook Fan page.

Reaction: The action by the brand needs to be followed by a reaction from the brand's interest group. The interest shown by the audience in the conversation and wall-posts that the brand has on its fan-page is often taken as the reaction from the audience. If users don't ignore or retaliate to the brand's presence online, that itself could be a good start.

Non financial impact: After the reaction stage follows the non financial impact of the action undertaken by any business. This may or may not translate into direct sales but surely will boost the brand image for any business. Examples of the non financial impact that a brand could receive are things like:

- 10,000 people like/share/join conversations on Facebook fan page
- Website visits increases
- 5 times increase in brand mentions
- 40% increase in positive sentiment

Financial impact: The final step in the flow will be the financial gains that a brand receives as a result of its efforts over a period of time. The 10,000 people who are now connected with your fan-page receive regular updates/information about your products. Over the next few weeks, if they happen to purchase products worth Rs.2, 00,000/- that is your financial gain. This financial gain is a result of all the above steps including non financial outcomes.

ENGAGING ON FACEBOOK, TWITTER, LINKEDLN, GOOGLE+ AND PINTEREST

After having discovered so much about the social media world, I think it is time that we embark on this journey of knowing the "how to" of some of the popular platforms in the social media world. While the popularity of each individual platform differs with each type of interest group, it lies upon you to discover what is it that is the happening thing among your specific interest group. When you begin to look for answers to your questions you may at some point find yourself wondering about what is it that any platform holds that is attractive to your interest groups. To give you a little more clarity on this, the below are some examples on what the audience love about a certain platforms and what keeps them coming back for more.

REASONS WHY CONSUMERS LIKE FAN PAGES

Some top reasons why consumers like fan pages on the Facebook platform:

i. **To receive discounts and promos:** The very basis of marketing is to provide great value to the consumers. From the consumer point of view what better way than to be able to enjoy the products or services across many brands with a dollop of having to pay less than the usual price. This surely means more value for the money that they spend on any product or services. In order to be able to enjoy benefits of receiving discounts and promos, the consumers look out for fan pages on the Facebook platform. This is one of the reasons for the popularity of fan pages on platforms like Facebook.

ii. **Tips and tricks to use products they own:** In an innovative strategic move, the brands look to promote their products or services as the ultimate multipurpose products or services. During this promotion effort, they let out valuable tips and tricks on how the products could be put to use in more than the regular ways. This is highly benefitting to those consumers who already are the owners of the product or services. They are enabled to discover more and more uses for the same product or services that they own. This translates into being able to get more value for the amount already invested in the product or service.

iii. **Quizzes:** Facebook offers a great platform for polls and quizzes for its audience. The consumers are at times lured by the great prizes that they could sweep away by taking part in these activities or they are also swayed away by the sheer excitement of taking part in these activities. With such activities buzzing on in the social media platform the consumer are surely left coming back for more each time.

iv. **Resolution of a problem:** Normal human tendency laws state that when we find ourselves amidst any kind of problems, we begin to look for answers and would turn to other people find the answers to the problem. Even on the social media world it is no different. When something is bothering the consumer, he shall look out for solutions that can come to him through the entire medium. When on this search for solutions, he will be delighted to be treated with solutions on the social media platform. That is what adds that extra scoop to the consumer for being a part of the fan page for any brand on the Facebook platform.

v. **Apps:** The lure of being able to have access and information about the great apps around different products or services is great for the consumers. The discussions around this happen on the fan pages of the particular brand on platforms like Facebook.

vi. **Games:** For those gaming addicts out there, fan pages provide a great platform to satisfy their gaming pangs. These fan pages also provide the consumer's a great place to boast about their scores and beat competition. This is the main reason why it is so popular among the young generations today.

vii. **Updates:** Receiving constant updates about the different brands or the products and services that the brand offers is a great way to stay informed about the ever changing world around. This is what the consumers think when the reach out to join those fan pages on the Facebook platform.

viii. **To show support for brand to friends:** Flaunting great brands has always been a hit among those brand conscious individuals of the society. With this trend on such a rise, it became inevitable that it catches on in the social media space as well. People turn to fan pages of the various brands that they would like to be associated with in the knowledge of their peers and friends. This shall help them boast their image as well. This is the reason why fan pages carry a lot of value for the brand junkies.

After having answered the question of why the consumers love the social media platform so much, let us now switch our view. Let us now see the social platform from the point of view of your business and what magic could be created with its help.

SOME OF THE COOL THINGS YOU CAN DO WITH FACEBOOK ADS
Target people on their birthdays

It shall always remain true that every person feels special about their own birthdays. When they are made to feel even special by somebody else, the relationship that is built grows stronger than ever. In order to benefit from this, you could reach the customer or prospect on their birthday, while they check their friends' birthday wishes on the wall. You can offer them a discount or surprise them by saying Happy Birthday from your brand. This is a small act that shall mean a lot to the individual and in turn will translate into a greater customer relationship management strategy for your brand itself.

Target your fans with reminders about cool events and promotions or just to say thank you

It is the new age strategy to actually build that great customer relationship by constantly keeping in touch with the customer. The reason for getting in touch could be anything like say reminding them about a cool event that your brand is organizing or the promotional offers that you are offering. You could get in touch with them to get their valuable feedback on any new innovation that your brand just rolled out into the market or just to say thank you. The reason could be anything but the importance lies on the fact that you would be focusing on keeping in touch always.

Target your employees

Whether you believe it or not, your employees are the most important asset to your organization. This holds true even when you are talking in context with the social media platform. Getting your employees to really talk about you over the social media space shall add credibility to your brand as well as give you access to the networks that your employees posses. Given that this could be so useful to you, you will also need to make sure you don't force it on to your employees. The act of talking about your brand should seem like a natural progression to them so that they are able to engage in it without feeling like they are being made to sell your brand. This shall help the brand a lot.

Build potential relationships:

Use Facebook ads to build potential relationships to help your brand foster great connect with the customer base. Target those people who have a need that your brand is capable of fixing so that it is easier to convince them about your brand. Due to the fact that they are already on the lookout for solutions to their needs they are mostly likely to be open to trying new brands and shall stick with them if they are satisfied enough. That is your cash in point.

Target traditional media:

Another great idea that you could make use of is to use Facebook ads to get connected with employees of leading media channels in your locality and introduce them to your company news. This shall help you get featured on various publications and magazines so that you are able to grab more attention from your interest groups.

Use 'sponsored stories' option in Facebook ads

One of the great options provided by the Facebook platform is the option to use 'sponsored stories'. This is one great way to communicate with your prospective consumer. Using the sponsored stories option you could get your message across to your customers without really looking like you are hard selling anything to them. This is marketing in disguise but nevertheless a very effective way to get your brands message heard.

After knowing what some of the social media platforms could do to your business, you are sure to be let thinking on how to get started on these new platforms that you wish to tap for great potential. As a matter of fact I would like to tell you that it is easy to discover the features of any social platform. Almost all have how-to videos for these features. These are dynamic in nature and new features are added almost every month. Hence, I will refrain from explaining various features of these platforms, and focus on how some of these could be used to engage consumers on social media.

HOW FACEBOOK HELPS YOU CONNECT
WITH YOUR AUDIENCE

1. Facebook hits right on target when it comes to helping brands know what is on their interest group's mind. It comes as no surprise that the kind of information that Facebook is capable of providing is worth more than any marketing survey that the brand might decide to pay for. When the source of information is so direct there is very less chance of misinterpretation and wrong action steps for the brand in question. Thus Facebook undoubtedly provides the best platform for fostering product development and innovation. It is definitely more than what any brand out there could possibly hope for.

2. Every marketing guru shall agree with me when I say that some of the greatest brands of all times have sworn by the most effective marketing practice which is the word of mouth way. Though the times have changed, the effectiveness of this practice remains just intact. And this practice is being taken to a whole new level by no other platform than the very popular Facebook platform.

3. When the channel that a brand uses is the one of word of mouth it surely works very well with developing preference for that particular brand in the minds of the consumer. The preference and differentiation that can be earned that way has a lot to do with being spread through trusted sources and speaking from experience. This differentiation will surely keep the brand in the limelight like no other source does.

4. With the Facebook trend catching on like wildfire with each passing moment the eyeballs glued to it also increases. This increase has benefitted everybody involved along with it. Thus there is no better way to increase traffic and also considerable increase in sales.

5. The basis of Facebook has always been about building and strengthening relationships. This basic value that the platform holds is also capable of getting caught by the brand that uses this platform itself. The brand is therefore able to build and also most importantly

sustain strong dependable relationships with the audience that shall benefit the brand the most.

6. The greatest boon of the social media platforms like Facebook has been the fact that a direct result of amplification of any efforts can be felt. These platforms offer amplification of recommendations and also word of mouth that is great for any brand. The brands are thus able to take benefit of greater results with lesser efforts put into it.

7. Facebook offers a great platform for any brand to actually gain insights about what the consumer feels about them and what are the needs that they express that can be met by their business.

ON THE ROAD WITH THE TWEET BIRDIE

When it comes to the tweet bird I think there are so many brands that have been successfully using them since long that it is difficult to actually pick the most successful of them all. That is the kind of success that is possible using Twitter. Talking in the Indian context alone, let us now throw some light on a few brands that have managed everything on Twitter.

Some prominent companies utilizing Twitter in India

1. **MTV** – The music channel has definitely caught the pulse of the young generation that is its interest group early and thus has been able to engage with them with the most effective ways available to capture the attention of the youth of the country.

2. **Hippo chips** – This brand stands as a shining example to how a brand grew its sales by 76% within a few months of its entry onto a social media platform like Twitter.

3. **Times of India** – This news giant redefined the way people receive their regular news updates. Using numerous ways to connect to the right audience to the brand, they have been able come a long way. Twitter is one of the platforms that the Times of India team decided to use while they were revolutionizing the news industry.

4. **Tata DoCoMo** – This is one of those brands that strived hard to

stay young and fresh since its inception. So where else do you expect they would look out to grow their network than the social media platform? Their journey over Twitter has been remarkable.

5. **IPL** – In a cricket crazy country like ours, it is definitely easy to pull a crowd to follow the game. Cashing in this great advantage and implementing it in the form of engagements over social media network, IPL has surely come a long way.

HOW TWITTER HELPS YOU CONNECT WITH YOUR AUDIENCE

After knowing how you could possibly put Facebook to work for your advantage, it is time you begun explore what the other social media platforms like Twitter have in store for you. Just as there are a lot of ways to make Facebook work for you, Twitter also promises to do many and many things for you. In order to enable you to dig in a little further, I have listed a few things that you could start doing with the help of Twitter.

Use the Hashtag(#) to Post Interesting Information Prior to any big event

I have surely said this before and will say it again "Start using the conference hash tags within your content". This is a tried and tested way for you to take while you are trying out the Twitter platform in order to make it work for you. You could start using the hash tags a couple of weeks prior to tweet information that is relevant to your audience. Searching around on the Internet under keywords that your audience might find interesting and then sharing that information accomplishes two things: it helps you learn more about your audience and it familiarizes your audience with you. If you are monitoring the hashtag, you will also probably see links to interesting posts. Re-tweet those that you think your audience would enjoy.

Pulling more crowds is what Your Session Should Focus On

You could arrange a session detailing what your brand is about in order to let more people know about you. While at it, it shall be helpful if you resort to putting into use the conference hashtag on Twitter, you can ask a question about what your audience might want to know for inclusion in your presentation. You can also do this on your Facebook page. You can respond to the answers on Twitter, again, using the conference hashtag and giving more exposure to the topic of your session. But save the best information for the session. Include a tweet saying something like, "For more on this topic, join me at my session" and include a link to your session in the online program.

Use Twitter to Organize or Join Meet-Ups with your brand's interest groups

Meet-ups are another great way to pull crowd attention and use it for your benefit. Any event is an opportunity for socializing and presenters who take advantage of this and make use of tools like social media to connect with people, can do much to ensure they are well received

Using the conference hashtag, you could send out a few tweets asking online followers to a Tweet Up or join a meet up that is scheduled. Often attendees are looking to interact and ask one-on-one questions of those who will be speaking about the brand. Making yourself available for this in a casual environment can help you in many ways. Knowing a few people in the audience can make it a friendlier environment for you and everyone there.

Ask your interest group to tweet Questions to you

Encourage your audience to use the conference hashtag to tweet questions. Some may prefer to just raise their hands to ask a question, but others who are more reserved, like the anonymity that tweeting provides and are more likely to engage that way. Answering tweeted questions has the added benefit of allowing you to interact with the remote audience at the same time you're interacting with the face to face audience. To ensure this process runs smoothly, ask somebody to monitor the conference hashtag during your presentation to alert you to questions or issues tweeted by your audience. That way, you won't have to keep interrupting your presentation to look at the Twitter stream.

Monitor the Event Hashtag and Continue to Interact After Your meet up

Once your session has ended, keep watching the conference hashtag Twitter stream and contribute whenever you can. If you are attending sessions yourself or enjoying good conversation with your audience, tweet about it. Or if you can't stay for the conference, re-tweet tweets of others that you think would be appreciated. This shows you're interested in the community, not just in your own brand.

After this knowledge gain, I am sure you would also be interested in knowing who else has been using Twitter successfully over the past years. Two of the most successful brands that have used Twitter as their communication platform have been listed here:

Dell

Dell makes the list of brands that have been successfully using Twitter right because of its effective use of Twitter for direct marketing. Dell created a unique connect account named the @DellOutlet Twitter account, which reportedly brought in $1 million in sales less than two years after its launch. Dell uses the @DellOutlet account to tweet deep discount messages and promotions. And do know that there is a person behind the Twitter account, which makes it seem more human and less automated. Dell offers a variety of other Twitter accounts for specific audiences, such as the primary @Dell account, Michael Dell's Twitter account (@MichaelDell), and the @DellCares account for customer service. In total, Dell lists 34 Twitter accounts on its website — all targeted to specific audiences, topics, and languages. Is that not a shining example to how much efforts the brand is taking in order to be able to conquer the social media space.

Starbucks

When initially the coffee giant Starbucks entered into the social media space not many were sure of what was their motivation to do so. But as they grew over this platform, the picture became clearer and clearer to all the people watching their progress. Their Twitter interactions are unique. The @Starbucks Twitter account is filled with two-way conversations between the brand and customers. Some promotional and corporate announcement tweets are included, but they're infrequent or meaningful enough that the audience accepts them without complaint.

Tweets with photos are common and add an entertaining visual element. Also, Starbucks monitors tweets that mention the brand name and responds to messages when it's appropriate. For example, customer complaints are often responded to with an apology, along with the customer service email address, so Starbucks can (in their words) "make this right." Another interesting way that Starbucks uses Twitter is for crowd sourcing suggestions and ideas. Through the @MyStarbucksIdea account, anyone can suggest an idea for Starbucks. It's a highly interactive timeline filled with great suggestions for the company, and a very cost effective form of brand building. This surely kept people wondering how the brand actually came up with something so fresh and innovative.

Now after we have seen what the two mighty social media platforms have to offer, let us set on discovering another platform – LinkedIn If you want to leverage LinkedIn's lead gen potential for your business as much as possible, here is how you need to go about it. Below are few ways that you could use LinkedIn to work for you:

Blog RSS Feed

There's a very simple way to populate your LinkedIn brand page with your business' content, and it's called your blog's RSS feed. This is used to keep your followers updated on any content that you might have posted on any of your blogs. If you're going to add your blog's RSS feed to your page, just be sure you're regularly updating your blog with content. A stale feed of outdated posts that shows you haven't updated your blog in months will likely do you more harm than good.

Adding blog's RSS feed to your LinkedIn page

To add your blog's RSS feed to your LinkedIn page, click the dropdown menu next to Admin Tools for your page's 'Overview' tab, scroll to the bottom of the page, and enter your blog's RSS feed.

News Module

This is one blessed feature that LinkedIn offers. It can be useful because it pulls in any news mentions of your company that LinkedIn finds on the web and features them in the right-hand column of the Overview tab on your LinkedIn company page. Adding this module is a great way to highlight the media coverage your company has earned, adding third-party credibility and validation to your page.

How to enable the news module

The option to enable news mentions to be displayed on your page is right below the option to add your blog's RSS feed while you're in edit mode of the Overview tab.

Company Status Updates

The company status updates that LinkedIn offer is a big win for marketers everywhere, but not many have been leveraging it. Just as marketers can post updates to their Google+ page and Facebook page timeline, they can also do so on LinkedIn. This gives marketers the opportunity to expose more of their content directly to their LinkedIn followers, who see status update content in their LinkedIn updates feed on their LinkedIn homepage. Keeping a frequently updated and engaging page is the best way to organically attract new followers and expand your LinkedIn reach.

Products/Services Tab

LinkedIn also provides the freedom to the marketers so that they can highlight their product/service offerings on a separate 'Products & Services' tab. Building out this tab is a great way to highlight and promote your products and services. But are your products and services the only things that you can highlight on this tab? Not true. You can also leverage this valuable LinkedIn real estate to feature your marketing offers such as webinars, ebooks, free trials or other content to support lead generation.

The other awesome capability offered through the product tab is audience targeting. LinkedIn enables you to create up to 30 distinct landing pages for specific audience segments. This means you can show visitors to your products tab different variations depending on the targeting options you set up based on that user's company size, job function, industry, seniority, and/or geography. So if you have various segments of products or offers suitable for different audiences, you can only surface the ones that are applicable to those users.

Videos on Products Tab

While you're editing your Products & Services tab, don't miss out on the opportunity to add a video! Use this space to explain your products, services, and value proposition in a video format, and if you're leveraging product tab targeting, you can add a different video for each tab variation you create. The only catch here is that any video content you use must already be hosted on YouTube; the video feature requires you to include a YouTube link for your video in order to display it.

Product and Service Spotlight

Another products tab feature worth mentioning separately is the 'Product and Service Spotlight,' which enables you to feature three scrolling, clickable banner images (640×220 pixels) near the top of your products tab. Again, if you're leveraging targeted product tab landing pages, you can choose different spotlight images for each variation.

Recommendations

LinkedIn provides users with the opportunity to recommend your business' products and services. This is also one of the reasons why it's important to add your products and services to your products tab. Without products and services, your LinkedIn page visitors would have nothing to recommend. When a LinkedIn user recommends one of your products or services, it's displayed on the individual detailed page for that product. The total number of recommendations across all of your products/services is also displayed on the main products tab on your page. This is surely a boon to your business.

Careers Tab

The final LinkedIn company page feature at your disposal is the 'Careers' tab. And while LinkedIn can serve as a valuable marketing and lead generation tool, one of its most powerful benefits is in its professional networking potential. Use the basic careers tab to advertise your current job openings. Want to take it one step further? Get more robust capabilities by upgrading your account to a Silver or Gold Career Page, which gives you access to a "full suite of features for promoting careers at your company, including a clickable banner, customizable modules, analytics on who is viewing the page, direct links to recruiters, video content, and more." If you choose the Gold Career Page, you can even customize up to five different versions of the page to display different content and job opportunities based on the viewer's LinkedIn profile. Think of it like targeted product tab variations, but for careers!

PROMOTING YOUR BRAND ON PINTEREST

Next up is another interesting social networking site called Pinterest.

How can you actually make Pinterest suitable to your business needs? What are the different things that this platform facilitates? Here are some answers to the above questions:

Pinterest is one platform that is known to be a visual social network. The social network model revolves around a lot of things like creating a pin board that highlights some of your best visual content.

A lot of big brands are taking notice of the power of online visual content for marketing.

If your brand has released an ebook or a white paper recently, you can take a screenshot of it and add it to a board that's a collection of papers. Do the same if someone from your team has authored an industry book. This will help you establish your thought leadership on Pinterest.

Start posting photos of your customers

Promoting your happy customers is a great way to create a positive sentiment around your brand. Encourage your customers to send you photos or take photos of them at their best moments and create a board of their smiling faces –perhaps using your product or service. Is that not adding a great personalized touch to your brand image? It surely is.

Create a User-Generated Pin board

By enabling other users to contribute their own pins to your pinboards, you open up a great opportunity to involve fans and customers in your marketing. Pick out a few of your top evangelists or customers, and create a board dedicated to their pins. That is a smart way to appreciate their efforts while acknowledging them on your brand page.

Create a Video Gallery

You don't have to limit yourself to pinning images; you can pin videos, too! Create a pinboard of some of the interesting videos your business produces along with relevant images.

Use Hashtags

Just like Twitter and Google+, Pinterest supports the usage of hashtags. Users can use hashtags to tag their pins and make their content more search-friendly. Make the most of it.

Feature Offline Events

Create a pinboard that features the best photos and video footage of any events you host to help you generate buzz and promote the next one.

ENGAGING YOUR AUDIENCE ON GOOGLE+

Google+ is a new yet fast growing platform that promises a lot for brands to grow along. It may not have as many users as Facebook, but it can still be a powerful force. There are a lot of things that a brand could do with Google+. Here are some examples on what you could do:

Pictures upload

Google + offers your brand the advantage of being able to upload pictures along with giving the option to edit them as well.

Tag others

To tag someone else on Google+ put a+ and then start writing their name. This is a sure fire way to get engagement since they will be notified if they are tagged.

Leave insightful comments

If you leave a memorable comment on someone else's post there is a good chance they will reciprocate the favor to your brand.

Now this is how you can use these various platforms to work for your brand.

CR80

THINK SOCIAL MEDIA, THINK SUCCESS, THINK ANALYTICS

Social media, the next best thing to computer technology, has been able to grab the eyeballs through its existence and its impact. But when we say this, do we have enough facts to support this statement? Of course we do, and the credit for this goes to metrics and analytics for the social media websites. Measuring the impact of social media websites became important for numerous reasons. Because people and brands were spending a substantial amount of time and money in preparing and implementing their social media strategies, it became necessary for them to find out if those strategies were even working in the right direction. An analysis would have helped these companies build better strategies and reach more people through the social networking websites.

Necessity is the mother of new inventions and innovations and this statement holds true for social media analytics as well. Social media tracking was made available to the people so that they can measure the effectiveness of social media for their business. Since its inception, social media analytics have grown in popularity and have improved manifolds. The data collected through analytics proves useful in finding out more about the customers' choices and preferences. Once the marketers know their customers, they can bring in products and services that the customers would like. Only those brands who have this data can experiment with new things as they would then be able to gauge success through social media tracking.

To be able to track the digital footprints of customers, it is important to first know what is to be measured. One can maintain a list of items that are to be measured and then compile a result to know the trends. Here are some of the things that can be measured on a social media platform:

- Users (active, inactive, fans, followers)
- Views
- Posts, discussions, comments, reviews and posts
- Feedback
- Video and audio uploads and plays
- Age, gender and location
- Reach
- Impact and influence
- Trends, hot topics and keywords
- Subscribers, bookmarks, votes, likes and shares

The pointers above can very well be used as benchmarks and can be used to find out how the digital marketing strategies are working out. For instance, if a brand wants to measure its social media effectiveness across different channels, they can revolve their digital marketing strategy around the number of mentions, number of positive and negative mentions, replies to updates and mentions, response to promotional offers and online transactions carried out by the people who were redirected to the website by social media websites.

With all these benchmarks available, some confusion around their usage is obvious. Sometimes, it becomes difficult to find out what can be measured using a metric. Once you know social media well, you can find it out yourself but it certainly takes some experience with these websites to be able to judge that. Here is a gist of what all can be measured on the social media websites and how.

TRACING LINKS AND CONTENT THAT YOU POST

Ok, so you posted three blogs in a day and around 6 tweets as a part of a social media campaign for your business or a particular product. How would you come to know if your hard work has paid off or not? Tools like Tracx, Gremln, HotSite and Buffer can help you find out if the links you posted are being clicked on or not. Through these tools you can also find out if your posts have been reposted and if yes, then how many times and how often in a certain period of time. Knowing how your content is being liked by the customers, you can improve upon the quality of the content.

IT'S ALL ABOUT INFLUENCING THE AUDIENCE

It is very easy to find out the number of clicks on a link and the number of reposts but what matters more than this is the influence your posts had on the audience. The posts or the content that you post on your profile should be able to drive action. Using specific tools, you can measure the actions taken by people who read your content or clicked on a specific link.

FINDING WHAT PEOPLE THINK AND SAY ABOUT YOU

When you start tracking the audience responses on your website or social media content, you get to know what people think and say about your product or company. This will also give you a sneak peek at how they view your products with comparison to other similar products in the market, helping you to improve upon quality or marketing techniques. There are certain tools like ThoughtBuzz and Tracx that can help you find out if you have sent out a positive message or a negative one by analyzing the sentiments of the users.

Here are examples of certain tools and their special characteristics explaining what all can be measured using these tools.

Radian6, Crimson Hexagon, Buzzstream and Klout

These tools offer insight into connections within the profile, the influence of the social media posts and strategies and the engagement rate. If you wish to know how you have influenced the audience, these are the tools that you can put to use.(Refer chapter 4 and 5)

Facebook (fan count) TwitterGrader, Klout

To know how many connections your profile page has and how much is your reach in terms of geography. These tools can help you find out the demographic details of the customers.

Social bakers, Alterian, SM2

Though it is important to know about how your strategies have influenced the audience, it is equally vital to know how active a particular brand or person is and how frequently have they posted and visited the social networking sites. Tools like Social bakers, SM2 and Alterian can help you gauge these characteristics.

Google trends, Webtrends, Ominiture

It is deemed necessary to have a strong landing page to where you can direct your customers from the social networking websites. You can check the bounce rate for your landing page using these tools. In a way, you will be gauging the potential of the home page or the website. These tools can also be used to measure the number and frequency of unique visits, number of pages viewed, time spent on each page and the referrer URL. The referrer URL is the one from which the visitors are being directed to the website. Knowing this would help you plan your social media marketing plans around the same URL.

Once you have ample knowledge about the tools and their functioning, you will never face any problem with getting out different types of metrics reports. Most of the reports would just need you to press a simple button and the work will be done automatically. If you use all the above mentioned tools, you might just end up having too much data on your plate. Beware, as this might lead to confusion about what data is to be used and when. The best thing to do is to mark a few pointers as the benchmarks, measuring which you can easily tell if your campaign has been successful or not.

Marketing in social media is not easy because of the number of competitors in the industry, presenting different options to the customers. Confusion about what to measure and what metric to use for it can be time-taking and you might end up losing some business. Here are some pointers that can explain you how different attributes can be measured and using which metric.

Branding is important for every business and likewise, it is also important to find out how branding has been working and what results it has been getting. When looking to measure this attribute through social media, you can use metrics like cost per acquisition, impressions and number of unique visitors to your website or profile. Like branding, the reach of public relations can be measured through re-tweets, referrals and number of times when the name of your business or website appears on the social media.

When making a profile on any of the social media websites, it is important to add an element of entertainment to your pages to keep the audience interested. Social media experts have claimed that people are more likely to view a page if it has some sort of entertainment element in it. If you have added that element to your profile, measure its effectiveness by finding out the number of page views and the time spent by the people on your website. This can help you find out if your idea is working out or not and if you need to change your digital marketing strategies.

Digital marketing strategies revolve around content. To track the content's effectiveness, one can measure the trackbacks, comments and posts on the social media page. Number of downloads, lead conversion rate and cost per lead can help you gauge the lead generation.

By measuring all these attributes, you can look towards your digital marketing campaign from a fresh perspective. There can be clients who are not interested in your social media ventures but this is where you have to find an opportunity and grab their attention. If you fail to do this, there's a chance that your competitors will do that and win over the clients. This is one reason why you should choose to monitor social media with the help of different metrics and analytics tools. Doing this will help you gauge marketing and branding and also get to know what problems your customers have been facing with your products or services; just another chance to improve upon your service offerings.

Though monitoring gives you all this information, it is just one part of the whole picture and there is a lot more the social media analytics tools can tell you. For your ease, here are the reviews for five such tools that are worth knowing about.

Reinvigorate

This social media analytics tool shows heat maps while displaying real-time web analytics. Through this tool, you can get page level, hourly, daily and even monthly reports about the social media websites. This tool works wonders for those who only trust real-time data to get all the details. If you wish to try working with this tool, you can now download a trial version of it. After using the trial version if you feel that this is the perfect tool you were looking for, download the paid version of it, prices for which start from $10 for a month.

SocialFlow

This tool has been introduced by the same people who brought TweetDeck and bit.ly. According to experts and people who have tried their hands on this tool, it works like magic by posting messages during a time when your audience is the most receptive. Before it does this, it optimizes the messages to make them more useful for the public. It also has the capabilities of measuring followers and re-tweets.

TwentyFeet

This tool can be used for aggregating social statistics from social media websites like Facebook, YouTube and Twitter. Working like a genie for you, this tool comes for a cost that you would never mind paying as its such a useful tool. You receive pings from this tool whenever any event is triggered.

Sysomos

This is one tool that has gathered praise from the users in a comparatively short span of time. Because of its features, this tool has become one of the best social media monitoring tools available. The main feature of this product is Heartbeat, which monitors social media in the real-time mode and offers graphics and snapshots from the online conversations on Social Networking sites

Other key features of this product are:

Dashboard   There may be other tools that have a dashboard but the one here is completely customizable. You can adjust its features as per your requirements.

Metrics Measurement   Through this feature you can get more information about sentiments and the amount of the social media activity. Once you have this info, you can then compare your performance against other businesses that are in competition with you.

Demographics and Geography   Though it is important to know how many people know about your business and talk about it, at the same time it is important to find out which country or region they belong to. This is one tool that can help you find this information about the users.

Key influencers   On the social media websites, there are some people that can help you drive conversations while there are some that discourage discussions and comments. With Sysomos, you can find out about these categories of people who are important for your digital marketing campaign and can bring positive changes in it.

Radian 6

If you have been in the social media business for some time, it is certain that you would have heard someone mention this name in context to monitoring the social media activities. Like Sysomos, this tool too does have a dashboard but this one enables you to view conversations related to your business and that too in real time. These conversations are then converted into graphics to make it easy for you to analyze and measure the results.(Refer chapter 4 and 5)

Key features of this tool are:

Coverage   This is by far one of the best features of this tool that it encompasses more than 150 million public sites which includes forums, blogs, comments, public photos, news publications and videos.

Integration of Web Analytics   This tool can link to Omniture, Webtrends and Google Analytics and by doing this you can get all the statistics that you want.

Sentiment analysis   Through this feature you can get to know if a positive word is being spread about you and your business over the internet. You can gauge the quality of the conversations through this tool and find out the reaction of the audience.

There are numerous tools in the market that can be used to find out how your digital marketing campaign is progressing. Available for a small price, these tools are easy to be used and can give you the actual picture that you would not have known otherwise. Who knew every reaction of the audience through comments, likes, conversations, blogs and downloads could be measured one day? With the coming of these tools, life of social media experts has become a lot simpler as they have all the data on their fingertips. As social media progresses, the number of tools and their features would also improve.

When thinking of analytics and metrics, certain tools score more than others as they are robust and powerful. Every tool can benefit you in one or the other way but it's you who makes a choice and decides what defines success for your business and digital marketing campaign. Once you know this, you will be able to choose wisely, the tools that fit your purpose and give information that help you define the future strategy for social media. We advise you to choose wisely between all these tools to find out information that you need. Make optimum use of these tools and define strategies that bring success to your ventures.

CRSO

USING THIRD-PARTY APPS
TO ACCELERATE REACH

Social media has covered the whole world like a cloud and has been flourishing everyday with new applications and usability options coming up. Due to the benefits that social media offers, not just individuals but businesses too have started using it for promoting their business and for getting to know their audience in a better manner. Social media applications have helped people all across the globe in managing the content on their profile pages. Apart from the applications that come with the social media websites, there are certain applications that are not related to social media but can still interact with it. If you are a regular on the social media websites, you would know how these applications work and in what forms are these available to the public.

Some of the most common forms of the third-party applications include:

1. Quizzes
2. Polls
3. Games
4. Software through which users can post content on their social media profiles using measures like a cell phone or any other web application

If you are wondering how these applications work, you should know that the social media websites offer permissions to program developers to create the third-party applications. The program developers get access to the social media platforms to be able to create these applications. Social media would not have been this attractive if there was no third-party application helping the users in making their experiences better. The program developers think of creative ways through which they can help the users to connect to the social media platforms using not just their computers but other devices such as mobile phones and tablets. All you need to use these third-party applications is a device for which the application has been built and internet connection to be able to connect to the website or the social media platform.

The program developers who create these applications aim at making these as useful as possible for the end users. To be able to do this, sometimes, the social media websites offer them access to the personal information of the users so that the applications can be personalized as per the users interests and thinking process. It is true that the program developers are also able to access the private information of the users while creating these applications. This is a necessary thing to do because it helps make the applications better and more personalized.

There are certain third-party applications that seek permission from the user to share their profile but the catch here is that the users might not know about the extent of the permission they are granting to these third-party applications. Most of the users are not aware of the fact that these applications are not primarily associated with the social networks and are from a third party. Apart from these third party applications, there are certain apps that do not follow even the basic policies and regulations that have been put in place for all the applications.

There will be times when one accesses the social media websites and does not even come to know that he is granting access to the third-party applications. These applications appear in-built with the social media websites but there are certain things to keep in mind while using these third-party applications.

1. See if the applications have been covered under the social network's privacy policy. There are a lot many applications that the social networks may not cover.

2. There is no guarantee that the third-party applications will be secure. If you are using any such application, there are chances that your private data like username and password gets stolen or reaches a third party that should not actually know about it. Be safe and careful while using such applications prepared by third parties.

3. Remember – If by using the third-party applications, your confidential information is leaked, the social networking website cannot be held responsible for it. The third-party applications are developed by separate network programmers and only get the permission to interact with the social media network. The social networks may not be keeping a tab on what these applications are doing to the users and thus all the responsibility lies on you if you incur any sort of a loss of data through some of the applications.

4. A certain amount of information is necessary for these third-party applications to perform their function. When you grant access to them to view your profile information, the application might just get access to more information than what is actually necessary for it to operate.

5. Some applications are designed in a manner so that they can gain access to the users' information. This is why it is always good to be safe than sorry while using the third-party applications.

6. Beware of the unauthorized third-party applications as they may leave viruses on your system. There are applications that carry malware and drop it to your system when you access it. By doing this, the application attacks the computer and can gain access to confidential information stored on it. Hacking through third-party applications is another possibility that the users should be aware of.

7. It is difficult to know what information these applications are gathering so make sure that you practice caution while using these applications.

Social applications are created in a manner that they make the best use of the power of social networks and the information they contain. If used correctly, the social applications can very well be used by businesses to reach out to their customers and other interest groups. Social applications offer a lot of advantages, some of which are:

1. Boosting brand's visibility
2. Helping customers engage more with the business
3. Make marketing campaigns effective and result-oriented
4. Changing culture to make it better
5. Increasing productivity of the business as a whole
6. Capture market through the use of social media

Not every social application will serve all these purposes; only good applications developed in the right manner and programmed to perform the right task can complete this task. You can differentiate between a good and a bad social application by measuring them against certain parameters. A social application can be considered to be good if it has all the qualities given below:

1. Ability to attract attention and then engage the customer
2. Look and feel that appeals to the customer
3. Visual elements that attract attention and make it easy to operate the application
4. Take-aways for the users. Users demand certain result out of these applications. An application can perform various functions like giving access to some data or giving out any information that is necessary for the business or the customer
5. Easy user-interface
6. Uniqueness. Designing a simple application that offers no value is of no use
7. Scalability is another unique characteristic that the users would love to have in a social application

APPLICATIONS CAN HELP YOUR BUSINESS TOO!

As the businesses are starting to realize the importance of social media as a powerful marketing engine, they are adapting to it and using it to accomplish communication and marketing objectives. It has been proved that small businesses are the one that look forward to building strong and long lasting relationships with their customers. The marketing techniques used by small businesses are very simple but varied. Now with the coming of social media as one of the marketing platforms, the businesses have started using social apps as well.

Mobile technology has developed manifolds and is now available at cheaper rates to most of the people across the globe. The social apps can now also be accessed through mobile phones and this is one reason why small businesses are focusing on developing such applications for their users.

There are a number of social apps that brands have used for social networking websites. Here are some of the examples that we came across.

- Less water app by Levis – this social app was attached to the bigger cause of saving water. By telling the audience that a Levis' jeans needs less water to be washed, the brand worked on generating awareness.
- Viral video campaigns were launched by Hot Wheels
- Polls and sweepstakes were launched as apps by Southwest Airlines
- Bud Light organized sweepstakes. This option has been leveraged by a number of brands because of the interest people show in the sweepstakes.
- If you are a regular at Facebook, you must have seen the Coca-Cola app wherein one was able to send virtual cola gifts to their friends. This app too has been leveraged by many brands as one of the many ways to let audience know about their products.

Engaging applications have been used extensively by brands. Through these apps, the audience or the fans are asked to submit photos related to a particular theme or topic. Other users or a particular community votes for the best out of all the submissions.

- Nike launched a video contest where in the users were requested to send across their videos where they were performing stunts. The videos were posted on the Nike page and then the people in the community voted for the one that was the best.
- Levis once launched an application to find the new face for their advertisement. They wanted a new voice and a new model for their clothing line for women. To find the right person, they invited videos from girls to be able to choose the best.

If your business has still not started using social apps, its time you realize their importance and start utilizing them in your marketing campaigns. You can take help from professionals who create and deploy these apps to work for your business and take it to newer heights.

သ၈